Gifts of
Self-Esteem

Gifts of Self-Esteem

by

Mary Jane Woodger

CFI
Springville, Utah

ISBN 13: 978-1-59955-020-6

Published by CFI, an imprint of Cedar Fort, Inc.
2373 W. 700 S., Springville, Utah, 84663
Distributed by Cedar Fort, Inc., www.cedarfort.com

LIBRARY OF CONGRESS CATALOGING-IN-PUBLICATION DATA

Woodger, Mary Jane.
  The gifts of self-esteem / Mary Jane Woodger.
    p. cm.
  ISBN 978-1-59955-020-6 (alk. paper)
  1. Christian life--Mormon authors. 2. Self-esteem--Religious aspects--Church of Jesus Christ of Latter-day Saints. I. Title.

  BX8656.W63 2007
  248.4'89332--dc22

                          2007000903

Cover design by Nicole Williams
Edited and typeset by Angela Olsen
Cover design © 2007 by Lyle Mortimer
Printed in the United States of America

10 9 8 7 6 5 4 3 2 1

Printed on acid-free paper

Table of Contents

Chapter 1
Combatting *the Ds*

I TAUGHT JUNIOR HIGH SCHOOL HOME ECONOMICS and still live to tell about it. Though I enjoyed a lot of things about teaching that age group, it is challenging, and I have a great admiration for educators who still teach adolescents. At the time, I was teaching as part of Utah state's curriculum for seventh graders, a class identified by the acronym TLC. When most think of TLC, the phrase "tender loving care" comes to mind. Sometimes in my junior high school classes, it was anything but tender loving care. The acronym actually stood for "Technological Life Careers." Part of the curriculum was to teach about self-esteem, including a one-day lesson plan with another acronym, IALAC, which stood for "I am lovable and capable." Each time I taught this lesson, I made tags with IALAC written on them and asked the students to wear them on their shirts during class. Typical of thirteen-year-olds, my students tore the tags up, used them for spit wads, or poked each other with the pins that held the tags on their clothing. After trying to control the wearing of the tags, none of those involved, including me, felt more lovable or capable.

I taught my students about self-esteem as best I could. I followed the guide, tried to be innovative, and even asked other teachers how they taught the subject; but in all honesty, after two weeks expounding on self-esteem, I doubt if my teaching improved any of my students' confidence. Junior high students are at a difficult age, and at times I did not handle situations as well as I should have, even as I taught about self-esteem. I have nightmares of the final judgment. I see myself at the judgment bar while one of my former students testifies, "This woman completely ruined my self-esteem one day when I was in the seventh grade and she was trying to teach me I was lovable and capable." After that experience, I became convinced it was impossible to instruct anybody on how to achieve self-esteem.

I had another experience with my own self-esteem when I came to Brigham Young University (BYU) as an inexperienced visiting professor that taught me a lesson. My first year as a BYU professor was hard. I lack the words to describe how hard it was. When I was hired, I was basically told, "We'll let you teach at BYU for a year and see how you do. If we like you, then we might let you stay on a more permanent basis." I especially felt insecure as I began to rub shoulders with men and women in Religious Education that I had admired as an undergraduate. Fellow professors began watching me teach from the first day I taught at the university. Every word I wrote was critiqued numerous times. At the end of the semester, I experienced for the first time student evaluations, where students were asked to anonymously tell me what they thought of my teaching. During my first year, I found an interesting phenomenon about myself in regard to those student evaluations. I could receive fifty wonderful evaluations, but when I would read one that was critical, I would completely forget about the positive comments.

During that first year, a seasoned full professor gave me this advice: "If you can just get a little bit thicker skin, then you will make it through to tenure." In other words, if you really feel good about yourself, then you should be immune to pricks and barbs. That is simply not true. We are human beings with hearts as well as minds. It hurts to be criticized and analyzed, even when our actions warrant improvement. Worse yet is the pain that comes from being scorned, disrespected, ridiculed, mistreated, neglected, exploited, abused, humiliated, or degraded. These two experiences taught me that having a thick skin or studying about self-esteem is not the answer to developing a good self-image or a celestial personality in embryo.

Brigham Young University Professor of psychology Richard L. Bednar, along with his colleague Scott R. Peterson, have defined self-esteem as an internal well being, an appreciation for self, "a sense of emotional security that allows us to function more fully, freely, and effectively in almost every facet of life." Self-esteem is related to everything that seems to make us better people. Those with high self-esteem are more adjusted, happy, successful, and confident and have better communication. "And the benefits of high self-esteem tend to be consistent, regardless of social class, level of achievement, or religious affiliation."[1]

No one would disagree with the conclusion that having self-esteem is advantageous, but there is much discussion about how self-esteem is developed. Some think that self-esteem is developed by those around us loving us enough. Another theory says that if you do something for yourself, such as buy a new car, get a makeover, or make a lot of money, then it will increase your self-esteem. Others declare that productivity is synonymous with self-esteem: hence, the more you can accomplish off the checklist on your day-timer the better you will feel about yourself. And some believe that popularity is the key to a healthy self-esteem. I believe these concepts are all inaccurate.[2]

Nor do I believe that self-esteem is achieved through association with others. In mortality, some people try to cultivate their own self-esteem by association, such as social climbers who try to advance by who they know rather than what they know. Family members sometimes try to achieve self-esteem from their parents', husband's, wife's, or children's accomplishments. I love this statement by Camilla Kimball, wife of the prophet Spencer W. Kimball, who certainly could have tried to receive esteem from her father's accolades, who was a world renowned scientist, or from her husband's Church positions. She disclosed:

> In all my life I really disliked only one person. It was a woman I could hardly stand to speak to. She was so sickly sweet, yet so self-centered. She had nothing to talk about except her husband and her children's great accomplishments. She had no life of her own and had such vanity in reflected glory. I find I cannot recall her without distaste. May the Lord forgive me.[3]

I love Sister Kimball's phrase "such vanity in reflected glory." Self-esteem is always lost in the reflections of others.

Our Heavenly Father and His Son are glorious personages who do not have self-esteem by association; it does not matter who does what—they are still secure. Our Father in Heaven has a wonderful self-image and a personality of celestial attributes, yet we know that He still weeps at the actions of his children (Moses 7:28–29). He is not immune to the feelings in His heart when we reject Him. Jesus also wept (John 11:35). They are beings who feel, but instead of feeling bad for themselves, they feel empathy for the son or daughter who is making poor choices.

Before we were born, we too had healthy self-images. We came to this life as William Wordsworth expressed, "trailing clouds of glory." [4] The fact that we chose to come to earth suggests we had great confidence in our capacity to succeed. We were confidant about returning to our Father in Heaven. The gospel of Jesus Christ helps us discover and re-develop the confidence we possessed as children of God before we came through the veil. "One of the great lessons of understanding our true identity as a child of God is that our personal sense of self worth can only be high. There are no born losers in God's frame of reference." [5] Many are aware of those on the earth today who have rediscovered that confidence, who seem to possess an eternal self-esteem. Those who possess such confidence do not usually boast of it, and I would suggest that those who do boast are still void of those attributes that embrace a celestial being.

Last Christmas I received a brag letter from a childhood friend who boasted of her life and accomplishments. I am sure many have received the same kind of Christmas greetings. Her Christmas letter was accompanied by a picture of her family meticulously outfitted in matching clothing, with a baby on her lap, and her five other children surrounding their handsome father. Below are some excerpts from her letter. I have changed their names.

> Barbie's kind, worthy, helpmate displays his beautiful talent of teaching others in priesthood meeting each week helping other's testimonies grow. Barbie truly enjoys attending Sacrament meeting with her six well-behaved children, especially when her husband sings solos in the choir. As she looks at his adoring face and hears his angelic voice, she falls in love with her eternal helpmate all over again.
>
> At home, Ken's favorite past time is to play games with his children or help Barbie change diapers or clean. Barbie is sure that most women are envious of having a husband like Ken.

Barbie was sustained as the Young Women President. These teenagers have never enjoyed Young Women activities so much. What a joyful blessing it is to serve! Barbie has also been raising money for the local elementary school and single-handedly collected over $1,000 to buy new playground equipment.

Barbie and Ken's life is nearly perfect; in fact they aren't sure that life could be much better.

You may think the above description of Barbie and Ken's life is what having a celestial self-image or eternal personality is like. When reading such whimsy, we may think living the gospel of Jesus Christ should be like an insurance policy, guaranteeing such success. Growing up, I too thought if I just kept the commandments, my life would turn out like the one described above. However, my life is nothing like this Christmas greeting. I have had some great moments, but they are not constant, and many experiences in my life have been far from whimsical. Most of the time I do not mind though, because the Lord tells us that he chastises those he loves (D&C 95:1). A lack of challenges may indicate that we are not spiritually growing, or worse, that Satan has control over certain aspects of our life. Right after I read Barbie's words last Christmas, I expressed my gratitude to my Heavenly Father for loving me so much. I feel a bit sorry for my childhood friend who wrote the Christmas letter because if she is not experiencing some challenges, she must not be very influential.

LDS psychologist Carlfred Broderick coined the phrase "the Gospel is not insurance against pain."[6] Broderick tells of an experience when he was invited to speak at a Young Women Standard Night as a stake president. A young wife and mother spoke right before him. This speaker brought her darling children and her handsome husband to the meeting and told the young women how wonderful her life was. Her concluding remark was that if the young women lived the commandments, they too would have a life like hers.

When the speaker finished, President Broderick stood up and commented, "I'm happy for Sister so and so who just spoke to you, but do not believe for a minute if you keep all the commandments you will live a life of bliss. The gospel of Jesus Christ is not insurance against pain, it is a resource to get us through the pain."[7] Brother Broderick went on to become a rather infamous writer in the Latter-day

Saint genre. One of my favorites is a talk he entitled "The Joy of Depression: Four Paths to Spiritual Survival."

You might ask, "How can there be joy in depression?" Most people would think that being depressed is far from being celestial; and, personally, I consider those moments when I have been depressed anything but joyous. But depression and discouragement may signify that we are preparing for joy ahead.

When individuals continually keep telestial commandments, they can become a target for Satan to attack them in other ways besides tempting them to break moral laws. The adversary often ambushes them with what I refer to as the "Ds." My list of Ds includes feeling any of the following emotions:

Depression

Despair

Despondency

Being Dismissed

Discouragement

Doubt

Being Discounted

Feeling Dead

It is easier for me to sin when I get the Ds. Satan knows when I am in "D-mode," and I am more vulnerable to the adversary's fiery darts.

The Ds are a sign of our times. We are told that in the last days men's hearts will fail them (D&C 45:26). Although heart disease is a major cause of death, men's hearts are also failing them spiritually and emotionally. That is why we have programs for addiction, hospital facilities for mental health, drugs for depression. Satan exists, and with him are a third part of the hosts of heaven who have become devils. Sometimes I feel I have 150 little devils personally assigned to me. Devilish spirits seem to surround me when I get up in the morning and look in the mirror. Sometimes, one of them tells me, "You have such a chubby, ugly body." I have learned to reply out loud, "At least I have a body." At such moments I am well aware that the War in Heaven still rages inside each of us.[8] Yet, Satan knows he will eventually lose the war, so why does he continue to fight and attack? What is his motivation? The answer to that question is found in 2 Nephi 2:27:

> Wherefore men are free according to the flesh, and all things are given them which are expedient unto man. And they are free to choose liberty and eternal life, through the great Mediator of all men, or to choose captivity and death, according to the captivity and power of the devil; for he seeketh that all men might be miserable like unto himself.

Satan knows that misery loves company. He does not want us to talk to happy people when we are feeling sad. He has a plan to divert every soul from our Father in Heaven's great plan of happiness, using every tool imaginable. He takes over our thoughts and feelings; he discounts our worth and camouflages our achievements; he anticipates our resistance and then uses all five of our senses to convince us that we are useless. Satan does not care how he gets us down or depressed, even using the most influential people in our lives to help create those awful emotions whose names start with the letter D. In addition, Satan seems especially to hound us with the Ds when the Lord is trying to stretch us. As Elder Neal A. Maxwell of the Quorum of the Twelve Apostles warned us, sometimes "inwardly and anxiously we may worry too that an omniscient God sees more stretch in us than we feel we have. Hence when God is actually lifting us we may feel he is letting us down."[9]

Elder Maxwell introduces another "D" word: we sometimes feel "let down" even by our Heavenly Father. We may even feel a little unprotected from trials, especially if we are doing something important for the kingdom of God. The Prophet Joseph Smith observed, "The higher the authority we have, the greater the difficulty of the station."[10] There is another "D" word you and I sometime experience: difficulties. Sometimes it may seem unfair. The more good we try to do, the more the devil comes after us and the harder the trials become.

Recently, I was talking to a friend of mine who shared, "Sometimes I think about what I have gone through and I know 'so and so' could have never handled it. It almost seems that God is punishing me for being strong." I would suggest that such stretching is not a punishment but rather experience with promise for better things ahead. However, it is hard to be patient in the winnowing process when we are in an emotional state and experiencing those Ds. At such times, irrationally we tell ourselves, "I am not as important as the woman or man next door." We question our value, comparing ourselves with others unfairly as we compare our weaknesses with their strengths.

Being bombarded with Satan's tactics, we sometimes distort our own sense of achievement. In our Latter-day Saint culture, it seems difficult to avoid criticism, both subtle and blatant. For instance, people may criticize families. As Sheri L. Dew, former member of the General Relief Society Presidency, has remarked, if you have eight children, you may be asked how you can take care of that many children. If you only have one child, you may be asked how long you have been married. If you do not have any children, you may be unfairly classified by yourself or others as a second-class citizen. If a husband is successful, then he may be accused of never being home. If a father attends all his children's events, some may ask why he is not more motivated in his career. Sheri Dew once commented that compared to what we do to each other here, the Final Judgment will be a piece of cake. She has counseled that we each have a unique mission and it is not for us to judge. We need to assume that everyone is doing their best. [11]

To combat the Ds, we would be much better as Latter-day Saints to focus on what is mutually shared in our lives instead of what is different. Our lives are filled and complicated. My life is more complicated than my mother's, and my mother's was more complicated than my grandmother's. We drive down the road with a pager beeping and a cell phone at our ear. [12] Such complexity and busyness leaves us more accessible to Satan's Ds and distorts our knowledge of who we really are and our knowledge of our true identity as sons and daughters of God.

Often in our cybernetic world where the rapid transmission of personal, financial, and medical data can take place in a few seconds, we are warned of being vulnerable to theft, fraud, and exploitation of identifying numbers. The theft of credit card, bank account, or social security numbers can have ominous consequences on our finances. However, Elder Robert C. Oaks of the First Quorum of the Seventy suggests that there is a much more severe form of identity theft. Elder Oaks instructs,

> I'm talking about something much more basic, and much more important than who the world thinks you

are. I'm talking about who you think you are . . . [and] the possibility of theft of your eternal identity. . . . Satan is totally dedicated to thwarting and derailing all of this marvelous plan of happiness, knowledge, and process. We know that one of his primary tools is to entice us to forget who we really are, to fail to realize, or to forget our divine potential. This is the cruelest form of identity theft.

Now, how does Satan do it? He's quite straightforward and predictable. First he attempts to prompt doubts in our minds about our divine potential. He cultivates doctrine of the world that implies that we are much less than we really are. He undermines our faith, and thus our self confidence in our ability to achieve our potential. And even if we do understand and accept it, he still cultivates this doubt. He strives to bring us to a mind-set in which we believe that we, individually, are not good enough to ever achieve our celestial goals. . . . He strives to make us forget who we really are by cheap, temporary imitations of true and lasting joy. He dims our memory and fogs our testimony. [13]

This fogging and dimming by the adversary upon our eternal identities is permitted by our Heavenly Father. In his great plan of happiness, God permits us to do many things of which he clearly does not approve. However, he has supplied each of us with weapons to combat this full-blown assault on the saving leaven of the earth: Latter-day Saint men and women.

These weapons were identified for me in a remarkable way when I started teaching the standard works; it was then that I realized how to obtain a healthy self-esteem and feel secure with our personalities or characteristics. Moroni, Paul, and Joseph Smith understood this concept as they received revelations pertaining to spiritual gifts. Self-esteem is given to us through spiritual gifts. It is in our development of those gifts, once we have discovered them, that we gain confidence. Elder Robert C. Oaks concurs, "In a world so filled with despairing souls, lacking a sense of personal worth, it is most uplifting to know that each one of us is endowed from on high with at least one spiritual gift." [14] The purpose of spiritual gifts is to enlighten and to edify, and especially those three most important ones—faith, hope, and charity—have a lifting effect.[15] Spiritual gifts are given to us so we can have peace in this life and feel secure when we experience disappointments, discouragements, despair, doubts, fears, or jealousies. President Boyd K. Packer, Acting President of the Quorum of the Twelve Apostles promises, "If you learn and earnestly seek the gifts of the Spirit, then you will be competent. The problems will be there, but . . . you will find a great solace and comfort and a great power will be with you all the time."[16] To seek spiritual gifts is not just a good practice that reaps great blessings such as competence, solace, and comfort; it is a commandment.

With his request that modern Saints possess spiritual gifts, Moroni gives a rather stern warning. He admonishes,

> For if there be one among you that doeth good, he shall work by the power and gifts of God. . . . I exhort you to remember these things [spiritual gifts]; for the time speedily cometh that ye shall know that I lie not, for ye shall see me at the bar of God; and the Lord God will say unto you: Did I not declare my words unto you, which were written by this man, like as one crying from the dead, yea, even as one speaking out of the dust? (Moroni 10:25–27)

In other words, Moroni warns, "I told you to get some spiritual gifts. I will be at the final judgment bar witnessing a discussion between you and your Heavenly Father. God will say to you, "The last thing this man wrote was to tell you to get the spiritual gifts and you don't have any. Why didn't you heed his counsel?""

Why are spiritual gifts so important? Because not only will the possession of spiritual gifts be a measuring rod at the last judgment, the possession of spiritual gifts is also vital to our happiness in mortality. That is why possessing spiritual gifts is the last subject Moroni addresses in the Book of Mormon. Our self-esteem, how we feel about ourselves, is dependent on our possession of those gifts. Spiritual gifts are the weapons to be used against Satan's fiery darts and the full blown blitz he is waging against Latter-day Saints. Spiritual gifts will combat the Ds. And although Satan wields some influence, it is minuscule in comparison to a woman or man of God who possesses spiritual gifts.

1. Richard L. Bednar and Scott R. Peterson, *Spirituality and Self-Esteem: Developing the Inner Self* (Salt Lake City: Deseret Book, 1990), 34 and 10.

2. Ibid., 34, 10, and 82–86.

3. Caroline Eyring Miner and Edward L. Kimball, *Camilla: A Biography of Camilla Eyring Kimball* (Salt Lake City, Deseret Book, 1980), 189.

4. William Wordsworth, "Ode on Intimations of Immortality, from Recollections of Early Childhood" in *Selected Poems* (London: Penguin, 2004), 159.

5. Robert C. Oaks, "Understand Who You Are," Brigham Young University Devotional, 21 March 2006, 6.

6. William Wait, *The Joy of Depression: Four Paths to Spiritual Survival*, Covenant Recording, 1981.

7. Ibid.

8. Garth L. Allred, *Unlocking the Powers of Faith* (American Fork: Covenant Communications, 1993), 86.

9. Neal A. Maxwell, *Lord, Increase Our Faith* (Salt Lake City: Bookcraft, 1994), 3.

10. Joseph Fielding Smith, comp. *Teachings of the Prophet Joseph Smith* (Salt Lake City: Deseret Book, 1976), 113.

11. Sheri Dew, *No Doubt About It* (Salt Lake City: Deseret Book, 2001), 97, 225, and 228.

12. Ibid.

13. Robert C. Oaks, "Understand Who You Are," Brigham Young University Devotional, 21 March 2006, 6.

14. Ibid., 4.

15. Bruce R. McConkie, *Mormon Doctrine*, 2nd ed. (Salt Lake City: Bookcraft, 1996), 314.

16. "New Mission President Seminar," *Church News*, 7 July 2001, 3.

Chapter 2

He Said It
in the Garden

IN THE GARDEN OF EDEN, ADAM AND EVE were told that Satan would have power to bruise their heels. I used to think that warning from our Heavenly Father was unusual. I have had my share of bumps and bruises over the natural course of life, but I have never experienced a bruised heel, nor do I know of anyone else who has either. Because of its placement on the body, the heel is seldom open to contact that would cause such an injury. Therefore, I am left to only imagine what it would feel like to have a heel injured. It would be irritating but not debilitating. People could still function in their daily activities if they had bruised their heel. What was the Lord saying to Adam and Eve? I would suggest the Lord was speaking metaphorically when he warned us that Satan could bruise our heels.

Often when the Lord uses feet as a symbol in scripture, he is referring to goals. In the English vernacular we also use feet to represent aspirations. We speak of putting our best foot forward, getting off on the right foot, or walking down the right path. By using the symbol of a bruised heel, the Lord is helping us to understand that Satan sometimes interferes with our goals. However, we can still reach our desired aims, even if the adversary puts a few barriers and bruises in our way.

Along with warning Adam and Eve in the Garden of Eden about bruised heels, the Lord also gives them a great promise. Through their seed Adam and Eve would have power to crush Satan's head. What would you rather have a bruised heel or a crushed head? We as Adam and Eve's posterity can crush Satan's head through faith in the Lord Jesus Christ. And as we have faith in the Lord Jesus Christ we become more like him, and we develop a celestial personality. The Apostle John tells us that it is necessary for us to become like our Savior: "When he shall appear, we shall be like him; for we shall see him as he is" (1 John 3:2). Moroni repeats the same counsel, "Pray unto the Father with all the energy of heart . . . that when he shall appear we shall be like him, for we shall see him as he is; that we may have hope; that we may be purified even as he is pure" (Moroni 7:48).

To become like our Savior we must know Him and know what He is like. Growing up I came to understand a few things about our Redeemer. For instance, I learned, that He is omnipresent. I knew He was always there. I also knew that He was omniscient, knowing everything. I also have come to know that He is the epitome of spiritual gifts, possessing all spiritual gifts and using them to bless us.

However, some spiritual gifts that are useful in mortality will be useless in the eternities, like the gift of healing. However, three spiritual gifts will be absolutely necessary throughout the eternities: faith, hope and charity. Elder Neal A. Maxwell identified these three spiritual gifts as being portable; we can take them with us. [1]

In mortality, possessing these three gifts will also determine our sense of self-esteem. As we examine our own personalities, we may wonder if we possess these spiritual gifts. The following quiz adapted from Church Education Speaker Anita Canfield may be helpful in identifying how much faith, hope, and charity we possess. Take the following quiz by simply answering yes or no to each statement as it applies to you:

1. Making friends is hard for me.

2. I am unhappy.

3. I feel afraid.

4. I avoid competition.

5. When I feel criticized, I get defensive.

6. I feel inadequate.

7. When others succeed or earn praise I feel inferior.

8. I rarely compliment others.

9. I am insecure about voicing my opinion or presenting my own ideas. [2]

By answering any of the questions above with yes, a correlating feeling can be associated. If you feel afraid sometimes, if making friends is hard for you, or if you get defensive when you are criticized, you are experiencing fear. If you feel unhappy or inadequate, avoid competition, or feel insecure about voicing your opinion, you are struggling with doubts. And if you feel inferior when others succeed or earn praise or rarely compliment others, you are jealous. You are experiencing the negation of these three spiritual gifts, the opposite of faith, hope, and charity, for the lack of faith is fear, the lack of hope is doubt, and the lack of charity is jealousy. On the other hand, believing is synonymous with having faith, having expectations is having hope, and love is the same thing as charity. [3]

As we become more believing, have expectations that the Lord will bless us, and love others with the pure love of Christ, our celestial personalities will begin to blossom and grow, and we will develop a self-esteem we have never known before.

1. Neal A. Maxwell, "The Precious Promise," *Ensign*, April 2004, 42.

2. Anita Canfield, *Self-Esteem and the Social You* (Orem: Raymont Publishers, 1982), 2.

3. Ibid.

Chapter 3
Faith Is First, Last, and
Everything in Between

FAITH IS ALWAYS THE STARTING POINT. It is the place we begin our testimonies and also the first step in developing a celestial self-image. There is a reason faith is the first principle of the Gospel. Faith brings our Heavenly Father and the Atonement fully into our lives. Faith narrows the distance between who we were, who we are, and who we will become. It is also the gate to personal revelation. We cannot have personal "revelation without first developing a personal faith in God's patterns of divine disclosure."[1] Faith is the principle of eternal increase. It increases wisdom, intelligence, honor, excellence, power, glory, might, and dominion. The attribute of faith fills eternity with creations. It is also the attribute that fills an eternal personality. Faith builds, lifts, and enlarges.

The adversary knows nothing of faith. Instead, the devil works on the principle of deception, enticing us to believe in things that are not true. This principle of deception destroys, dissolves, decomposes, and tears in pieces our hopes, dreams, and self-esteem. Deception wreaks destruction on marriages, friendships, and any purposeful lifting in all of its dimensions. The deception the adversary works with is weak compared to faith in the Lord Jesus Christ, but if we let him, the adversary can weaken our ability to have faith.

In order to more fully understand faith, we must understand its opposite, which is fear. Joseph Smith clarified, "Where doubt and uncertainty are there faith is not, nor can it be. For doubt and faith do not exist in the same person at the same time."[2] Fear causes many problems and, ironically, often will come into existence when we are trying to exercise faith. Elder Jeffrey R. Holland of the Quorum of the Twelve observes:

> Opposition . . . often comes *after* enlightened decisions have been made, *after* moments of revelation and conviction have given us peace and an assurance we thought we would never lose . . . *God will also provide the means and power to achieve that purpose.* Trust in that eternal truth. If God has told you something is right, if something is indeed true for you, *he will provide the way for you to accomplish it.* That is true of joining the Church. It is true of getting an education, of going on a mission or getting married or of any of a hundred worthy tasks. [3]

If we fail to trust in eternal truth, as Elder Holland suggests, and let fear rule us, we will not only lose self-esteem, but we will also fail to accomplish what we were sent here to do.

In God's personality there is no fear; rather, He is the author of peace. Paul tells us, "For God hath not given us the spirit of fear; but of power, and of love, and of a sound mind" (2 Timothy 1:7). That spirit of power or a sound mind is faith. This does not mean that those who have faith in the Lord Jesus Christ will not experience trials and tribulations. Rather, a disciple of Jesus Christ learns to face turbulence with faith that brings power to overcome struggles. One who faced trials with faith and experienced great power was the mother of Elder Dallin H. Oaks of the Quorum of the Twelve Apostles.

Some would consider Dallin Harris Oaks' childhood tragic; however, somewhere as a boy Elder Oaks gained faith that sustained him. During the Great Depression, when Elder Oaks was just seven years old, his father died leaving behind a wife and three small children. Elder Oaks' mother, Stella Oaks, had a difficult time losing her husband and suffered a nervous breakdown. Subsequently, Dallin and his siblings were sent to live with grandparents.

One can imagine that Stella Oaks might have been judged negatively by some because of her reaction to her husband's death. Someone might have accused Stella Oaks of having a weak testimony or felt she was a poor mother to send her children away. One might imagine a well-meaning ward member saying to her: "You just have not prayed hard enough, or you would make it through this. You need to trust your Heavenly Father and his plan for you. He must have needed your husband more on the other side." I imagine "the Ds" were taking over Stella Oaks at the time.

The death of his father and his mother's nervous breakdown had a devastating effect on Elder Oaks. Later he remembered:

> I had a lot of problems in school . . . I just couldn't concentrate. I remember when we were learning how to do long division. We had to do 20 long division problems a day. Your score was how many you missed. My scores were always around 15 or 16. Looking back on it, I'm sure my problems were due to the emotional disturbance of losing my father and mother at the same time. But as far I was concerned at the time, I was the dumbest boy in the world. [4]

After Elder Oaks lived with his grandparents for two years, his mother recovered, began teaching school, and reunited with her children. I am sure those first few years after Stella Oaks reunited with her children, she did not go to Dallin's school teachers with Dallin in tow and say, "Well, I know why Dallin is the dumbest boy in class. Three years ago his dad died and I had a nervous breakdown and here is a crutch, Dallin; use it for the rest of your life and you can blame me for all of your problems." Sometimes as a secondary school teacher, I heard some parents do exactly that at parent-teacher conferences. I am sure Stella Oaks approached parenting differently because I have never heard Elder Oaks complain that he was somehow cheated out of a childhood or that during his most impressionable years he was abandoned.

At some point after Sister Oaks recovered, she used the experiences she and her children had been through as a rung on a ladder in reaching for the next part of their lives. The rung of faith she gave her son is described below. Elder Oaks recalls that he

> never felt tempted to drink or smoke while growing up because he couldn't bear to violate his mother's trust on things he knew were important to her. "There were plenty of things my mother hadn't thought of, and I found plenty of trouble to get into . . . but on things that were really important, there were no mistakes." . . . His feelings about prayer are also rooted in

his early home life, in the prayers his mother used to offer. A woman of immense faith, she would call on the Lord with perfect confidence when special blessings were needed. . . . She would review in her prayers their commitments and covenants, almost reminding the Lord that we had paid our tithing and offerings, that the desired blessing was, as nearly as we could judge, a righteous desire, . . . and that now we were laying hold on the Lord's promises. . . . Because my mother had no doubts about the Lord's reality and his ability to answer her prayers, I haven't either. [5]

Notice that Elder Oaks does not identify his mother as a woman who had a nervous breakdown; rather, he remembers her as a woman of immense faith. The Oaks' faith was based on prayer and their ability to receive answers from Heavenly Father. If we want to increase our faith we, like Elder Oak's mother, must increase our ability to receive answers to prayers and make things happen. Faith does make things happen. Elder Gene R. Cook of the First Quorum of Seventy observed the following:

Someone said long ago, when great events occur, there are three types of persons manifested: First, the one who doesn't realize that anything great is happening; second, the one who realizes something is going on but doesn't know what it is; and third, the one behind the scenes making it all happen. [6]

How does a person make things happen? How can someone be effective as a young man or woman, father or mother, or Church leader? They can change circumstances through faith in the Lord Jesus Christ. Faith is the force by which the Savior and our Heavenly Father make things happen. The Prophet Joseph Smith understood this concept when he instructed:

Had it not been for the principle of faith the worlds would never have been framed, neither would man have been formed of the dust. It is the principle by which Jehovah works, and through which he exercises power over all temporal as well as eternal things. Take this principle or attribute—for it is an attribute—from the Deity, and he would cease to exist. [7]

It is also interesting to note what the Prophet Joseph Smith said about the origin of faith among Adam and Eve's children:

> We have now clearly set forth how it is, and how it was, that God became an object of faith for rational beings; and also, upon what foundation the testimony was based which excited the inquiry and diligent search of the ancient saints to seek after and obtain a knowledge of the glory of God; and we have seen that it was a human testimony, and human testimony only, that excited this inquiry, in the first instance, in their minds. It was the credence they gave to the testimony of their fathers, this testimony having aroused their minds to inquire after the knowledge of God; the inquiry frequently terminated, indeed always terminated when rightly pursued, in the most glorious discoveries and eternal certainty.[8]

The type of faith that Jehovah used to create this world, which is eternally certain, are the kinds of faith President Boyd K. Packer describes below:

> There are two kinds of faith. One of them functions ordinarily in the life of every soul. It is the kind of faith born by experience; it gives us certainty that a new day will dawn, that spring will come, that growth will take place. It is the kind of faith that relates us with confidence to that which is scheduled to happen. . . .
>
> There is another kind of faith, rare indeed. This is the kind of faith that *causes* things to happen. It is the kind of faith that is worthy and prepared and unyielding, and it calls forth things that otherwise would not be. It is the kind of faith that moves people. It is the kind of faith that sometimes moves things. Few men possess it. It comes by gradual growth. It is a marvelous, even a transcendent, power, a power as real as and as invisible as electricity. Directed and channeled, it has great effect.[9]

Such a faith as described by President Packer is an attribute of self-esteem and part of eternal self-confidence. It is also a component necessary for a successful mortality. Moroni tells us, "And now I come to that faith, of which I said I would speak; and I will tell you the way whereby ye may hold upon every good thing" (Moroni 7:21). Faith is power. If we are full of faith in the Lord Jesus Christ, we can obtain good things and literally cause things to work for good in our lives and in the lives of others. With the importance of faith in mind, we might ask how we can increase this wonderful power. One way to increase faith is by receiving answers to prayers.

Think of something where you need the Lord's help. You may have a wayward child, a difficult family relationship, a financial debt, a spouse involved with pornography, or a friendship that needs mending. Prayer can change a situation that would not change without the Lord's help. In order to receive the Lord's help, we can follow six steps fashioned by Elder Gene R. Cook in his book *Receiving Answers to Our Prayers*. [10] By following these six steps, I have had some wonderful experiences with increasing the power of faith in my own life.

Step 1:
Faith in the Lord Jesus Christ

Having faith is always the first step in receiving answers to prayers. Faith in the Lord Jesus Christ is not synonymous with simply having a positive mental attitude. Instead, it is having faith in a person, even God. That person to have faith in is not yourself. It is a relief when we can start to have faith in God instead of in ourselves. The responsibility to be confident or gain self-esteem on our own just does not work, but having confidence in our Savior has the side effect of also increasing our sense of self-worth. In *Lectures on Faith* number three, we are taught that in order to have faith in God, even the Lord Jesus Christ, we need to have three components in place.

First and foremost, to have faith in the Lord Jesus Christ one must understand His character. Elder Neal A. Maxwell warned that "poorly defined faith not only produces little conviction but also is difficult to nurture and increase." Faith involves much more than "an intellectual acknowledgement or even an appreciative admiration of [Jesus Christ]." [11] We cannot increase our faith without an increased understanding of Jesus Christ's character. We have to understand some absolutes about Jesus Christ in order to have faith in Him. These poignant characteristics of Jesus Christ's personality are listed in *Lectures on Faith* number three under six headings as follows:

> First, that he was God before the world was created, and that he was the same God after it was created.
>
> Second, that he is merciful and gracious, slow to anger, abundant in goodness, and that he was so from ever-lasting and will be to everlasting.
>
> Third, that he changes not, neither is there variable-ness with him: but that he is the same from everlast-ing to everlasting, being the same yesterday, today and forever; and that his course is one eternal round, with-out variation.
>
> Fourth, that he is a God of truth and cannot lie.
>
> Fifth, that he is no respecter of persons.
>
> Sixth, that he is love. [12]

Without understanding each of these attributes, faith can be pro-hibited. For instance, we might ask ourselves, "Do I understand that He knows my past and everything about me and what I need to do?" He is the only one who knows the end from the beginning and knows step by step how to get you and me back home. A prayerful life is based on trusting that perspective.

The God we pray to is "merciful and gracious, slow to anger, [and] abundant in goodness." [13] His Son is also abundant in that same good-ness that He "came not only to save us from our sins, but also to assist us with our infirmities, our afflictions, our weaknesses, our problems, and our discouragements." [14] He wants us to be happy. That knowledge entails believing not only in His macro–plan of salvation but also in His micro-plan for our personal lives. [15] Elder Robert C. Oaks of the First Quorum of Seventy informs, "It is a sweet blessing . . . to know that he has a plan with an exalted purpose for each of his children. It is also a very powerful personal driver to be able to accept that we each have a particular role to play in this plan." [16] Without that trust and knowledge, we will never be able to pray with power.

"He is a God of truth and cannot lie," and because He cannot lie He keeps promises both globally and personally (Ether 3:12; see also Alma 37:17). "He is no respecter of persons" (D&C 38:16) [17] He wants you to be just as happy as your neighbor, your bishop's wife, or the university professor. As Elder Henry B. Eyring of the Quorum of the Twelve reiterated, "Faith is not simply to know God *could* do something. Faith is to know He *will*." [18] If we doubt whether the Lord will reveal His will to us, then He probably won't. The Stripling Warriors were able to receive the wonderful blessing of divine protection because they did not doubt their knowledge of God's nature (Alma 56:48). Such reassurance is repeated in this powerful promise found in modern scripture:

> Your prayers have entered into the ears of the Lord of Saboath, and are recorded with this seal and testament—the Lord hath sworn and decreed that they shall be granted.
>
> Therefore, he giveth this promise unto you, with an immutable covenant that they shall be fulfilled. (D&C 98:2–3)

In these verses the Lord seals, testifies, decrees, and gives an immutable, non-reversible covenant that He answers all prayers, including yours and mine.

We must also know that "He is love." [19] As Paul tells us, nothing we can do can separate us from God's love; not tribulation, distress, famine, nakedness, peril, death, life, angels, or principalities can make Him stop loving me or you. No height, depth, or any other creature, including ourselves, can separate us from that great love (Romans 8:31–39). With that love in place, you and I do not have to worry about anything that will happen on this trail of life. We can proclaim with pioneer William Clayton that there is "nothing to fear from the journey." [20]

In the past, when I looked over the list of divine attributes, I understood and believed that God had all of these attributes—except for one. As a child I understood that Jesus was omnipresent, that he was always available. I also accepted omniscience—I absolutely believed that Jesus Christ knew everything, including everything about me, my past, present, and future. The one attribute I misunderstood was Jesus Christ's omni-loving nature. In my early adult life, I did not believe Jesus Christ's personal plan for me would make me happy. Believing He was a harsh God dishing out a "tough love" to bear under, I was devoid of accepting His love for me. Such a misunderstanding of His characteristic love brought a great deficit in my trust of Him, and until

I understood His loving nature, my faith was limited. In looking over the other five characteristics headings, you may find other attributes that you misunderstand that impedes your faith.

Second, we are told that in order to have faith we must know that Jesus Christ exists. Moroni tells us that he knows that the Lord "workest unto the children of men according to their faith" (Ether 12:29). Although the lyrics were later changed by President Spencer W. Kimball to emphasize that this is a gospel of action, many primary children sang, "Teach me all that I must know to live with him some day."[21] The most important knowledge we need in order to produce efficacious and productive prayers is that our Heavenly Father and the Lord Jesus Christ exist. They are real and we have a relationship with both of them.

Although the Lord has promised to grant our righteous desires, the miracle of prayer does not reside in our ability to manipulate situations and events. Rather, the miracle is that we are in a relationship with a God and have the knowledge that He is there.[22] Do you truly know that he is omnipresent in your life? President McKay explained how we can feel that presence:

> In secret prayer go into the room, close the door, pull down the shades and kneel in the center of the room. For a period of five minutes or so, say nothing. Just think of what God has done for you, of what are your greatest spiritual and temporal needs. When you sense that, and sense his presence, then pour out your soul to him.[23]

Third, we must have "an actual knowledge that the course of life which [we are] pursuing is according to his will."[24] In President Kimball's language, we must know we are worthy to receive answers to prayer and receive faith.[25] Some confuse being worthy with being perfect. However, such knowledge does not mean we have become perfect in our actions, behavior, or attitudes. Elder Neal A. Maxwell explains, "The Prophet Joseph Smith said we need to know 'that the course of life' we are pursuing 'is according to the will of God, in order to . . . exercise faith in him unto life and salvation.' Obviously, our imperfections make God's full and final approval of our lives impossible now, but the basic course of our life can be approved. If we have that basic reassurance, we can further develop faith."[26] I equate knowing our lives are in accordance with His will with being worthy—temple worthy. If Latter-day Saints can answer the temple recommend questions affirmatively, they are worthy of the Lord's blessings. That is all He requires to know that our path of life is in accordance with His will.

Step 2:
Paying a Price

It is difficult to hear the Lord when we are experiencing negative emotions such as anger, whether at the Lord, another individual, or the whole opposite gender. Elder Gene R. Cook tells us that "you can't hear the voice of the Spirit when you're mad."[27] Experiencing anger, contention, revenge, bitterness, or resentment is not conducive to prayer. Nor can we be full of lust or pride and still expect answers. In order to receive answers to prayers, we have to humble ourselves and make our hearts right. The price we pay for answered prayers is internal, a willingness to change or sacrifice. The Prophet Joseph Smith showed us one way to pay a price, and receive answers to our prayers. In one account of the First Vision, Joseph Smith said that he went to the grove "for my own sins and for the sins of the world."[28] Joseph's worst fear was that he might offend God (JS—H 1:25). He had his heart right with the Lord before he asked for answers to his prayers.

Another way to describe such actions is repentance. When seeking a blessing or an answer to prayer, we may go to the Lord and ask, "What is standing in my way of receiving this blessing?" He will then tell us what we might need to change in our lives. In many of our approaches to repenting, one problem may incur—we may think of repenting in grandiose terms. Unless the hairs on our arms rise up or we flood our closets with tears, we sometimes feel that we have not repented. Someone once said that repenting is about as exciting as watching grass grow. Though the process may be slow, the results of repentance can be dramatic.

Increasing faith, therefore, requires decreasing one by one our personal equivocations, reservations, or hesitations. If we are reluctant to change, we will diminish our faith. Such reluctance can include refusal to work meekly at making a marriage succeed or a family happier, resentment of personal trials, or trying to serve the Lord without offending the devil, as President James E. Faust of the First Presidency has coined. [29] Neglecting prayer, scriptures, neighbors, Sacrament meeting, or temple attendance or following worldly ways slows the growth of faith. Whatever small sins we hold onto can impede faith; repentance, on the other hand, advances faith. Elder Gene R. Cook suggests:

> Suppose you are a mother or father with a son who is straying from the path of righteousness. I believe you can do much to pray him home. You can do much to fast him home. You can repent enough of your own sins that, through your sacrifice, the Lord may intervene more in his life and save the boy. It's not that your paying for your own sins—Jesus did that. But through your agency, through your sacrifice, you are able to receive blessings that you otherwise would not be able to obtain. [30]

As Elder Cook suggests, most often paying the price to receive answers to prayer comes by repentance and fasting. Fasting seems to get the Lord's attention quicker than other efforts. Fasting's effectiveness increases especially if you can get someone else to fast with you, such as a family member, friend, or a visiting teacher and will increase your power and ability to receive answers. Like lifting a large box where more people lighten the load, lifting our voices to heaven together in the attitude of fasting hastens answers.

Furthermore, meekly submitting to ordinances also constitutes a way we can pay a price. An open submitting to authority as held by those God has called to administer thus increases our faith. Asking, seeking, then following guidance from local priesthood authorities is also a form of paying a price that brings great revelatory blessings.

Another way to prepare for blessings is to offer more obedience than we are now doing. If we are anxious to have specific revelations and new blessings come into our lives, we can increase our worthiness by keeping the commandments with more exactness. The Stripling Warriors, who constitute one of the best scriptural accounts of faithfulness, "did obey and observe to perform every word of command *with exactness*; yea, and even according to their faith it was done unto them" (Alma 57:21, emphasis added). If we obey and observe with exactness all counsel, including that given to us by local leaders, the Lord will do unto us according to our faith also. Another price to be paid is praying as if everything depends on Him, for ultimately it does.

Step 3: Pray Like Everything Depends on Him

I have learned some simple things about prayer that have made all the difference in my ability to receive answers. President Kimball instructed, "If you want the blessing, don't just kneel down and pray about it. Prepare yourselves in every conceivable way you can in order to make yourselves worthy to receive the blessing you seek." [31] Discussing the subject of prayer more regularly can prepare us for communication with our Father in Heaven. President Hinckley observes: "The trouble with most of our prayers is that we give them as if we were picking up the telephone and ordering groceries—we place our order and hang up. We need to meditate, contemplate, think of what we are praying about and for." [32] To paraphrase 2 Nephi 25:26, we should be talking of prayer, rejoicing in prayer, preaching about prayer, prophesying about what we learn in prayer, and writing down what we pray about. Through Isaiah, the Lord said, "Come now, and let us reason together" (1:18). Part of my preparation when I really need a blessing from the Lord is to go to those I respect and love and ask, "How should I pray about this?" Talking about prayers brings me more power in prayer. I have found if we converse more about prayer, we will be more focused and receive more insight about those concerns we pray about.

We are promised that we are not alone in prayer; we will be given what to say if we will meditate and contemplate (3 Nephi 19:24). The true way to pray is to repeat what the Spirit utters. The best place for me to practice letting the Spirit direct my prayers is in my stewardship as a visiting teacher. Usually, I have no selfish interests in that situation, and it is easy to let my mind be filled with what the Spirit has to say. I feel disappointed when my own visiting teachers give a generic prayer in my home and simply bless that I will have a good month. I need them to pray for and in my behalf. As I have done that for and in behalf of those I visit teach, it has spilled over to my private prayers, and with that practice, I am learning what to say in my personal prayers through the Spirit.

Prayer should be a vital, on-going process at the heart of our daily lives. President Kimball instructs below about the place of prayer in our lives:

> We always have a prayer in our hearts that we may do our best on the football field, that we may appear well in the classroom, that we may remember the things we have learned when the test is on, that we may be impressive to our friends. We pray as we stand to speak, as we walk, as we drive. We remember our friends, our enemies. We pray for wisdom and judgment. We pray for protection in dangerous places and for strength in moments of temptation. We utter momentary prayers in word or thought, aloud or in the deepest silence. Can one do evil when honest prayers are in his heart and on his lips? [33]

The last line in this quote speaks of having a prayer on our lips. There is great power in praying aloud. If we really want the Lord's attention, we should let Him hear the words of our mouths, even praying vocally when we are alone. Fourteen-year-old Joseph Smith had surely prayed before, but not vocally till the First Vision (JS—H 1:14). Moreover, praying aloud is not just a good idea, it is a commandment. In section 19 of the Doctrine and Covenants, Martin Harris is commanded to pray aloud (vs. 28), and Joseph Knight was directed to "pray vocally" in section 23 (vs. 6).

Vocal prayer is powerful. It helps us concentrate thoughts and subsequent actions. The scriptures are replete with those who lifted their voices to the heavens. Nephi prayed aloud (2 Nephi 4:24), Enos raised his voice till it reached the heavens (Enos 1:4), and Alma and his people prayed so loud that their captors said if they did not stop they would be put to death (Mosiah 24:10–12). Christ offered his great intercessory prayer aloud (John 17:1), and His prayer in the Garden of Gethsemane was audible (Matthew 26:39–44). If at all possible, when we are on our knees, praying aloud is advantageous.

Along with being commanded to pray aloud, we are also commanded to be united in prayer (D&C 29:6). Obviously, that commandment includes praying unitedly as families. Elder Gene R. Cook promises,

A family united in prayer can have real spiritual power because of their faith. I honestly believe that if a family is praying for what is honorable and right, they have every right to assume that the Lord will respond to them. He will either bless them with what they desire or give them some indication of why they cannot have it, or indicate that they ought to quit praying for something they will not receive. [34]

That is a great promise for those who have families. However, right now I live alone. Yet, those great promises that come from praying together can apply to me also: "Whatsoever ye shall ask in faith, being united in prayer, according to my command ye shall receive" (D&C 29:6). I have found a few wonderful brothers and sisters in the gospel who are like-minded, who want the same blessings, and it has been a wonderful experience to pray aloud with them. When you "agree . . . as touching anything that [you] shall ask," powerful answers result (Matthew 18:19 and D&C 42:3). When two or more are gathered in His name praying aloud together, He is there also, and great prayers ascend to heaven.

As we pray together, it is also important to admit our weaknesses to the Lord. Look how the brother of Jared begins his prayer that brought the Savior's appearance by admitting weakness:

> Behold, O Lord, and do not be angry with thy servant because of his weakness before thee; . . . we are unworthy before thee; because of the fall our natures have become evil continually; nevertheless, O Lord, thou hast given us a commandment that we must call upon thee, that from thee we can receive according to our desires. (Ether 3:2)

Like the brother of Jared we too can receive the desires of our hearts if we are willing to confess weakness to the Lord. President Kimball reiterates:

> We confess our weaknesses. We plead for help to overcome and for forgiveness of our transgressions, our evil thoughts. We bare our souls. Can anyone long have an enemy or continue to hate one for whom he prays? Here one sheds all pretense, sham, deceit. He stands

before his maker as he really is, without affectation, or
subterfuge. . . . In your secret prayers do you present
yourself with your soul bared, or do you dress yourself in fancy coverings and pressure God to see your
virtues? Do you emphasize your goodness and cover
your sins with a blanket of pretense? Or do you plead
for mercy at the hands of kind Providence?[35]

As President Kimball explains, admitting mistakes is prerequisite to
receiving mercy from our Father in Heaven.

After confessing our weaknesses, we can then ask for the desires
of our hearts. James writes that sometimes we have not because we ask
not (James 4:2). The Lord informs us that He knows what things we
need before we even ask (Matthew 6:8). An important question to ask
is, "If he already knows what I need, why does he require that I still
ask?" The Bible Dictionary answers that question: "Prayer is the act by
which the will of the Father and the will of the child are brought into
correspondence with each other. The object of prayer is not to change
the will of God, but to secure for ourselves and for others blessing that
God is already willing to grant, but that are made conditional on our
asking them."[36] As Virginia H. Pearce recently suggested,

> Prayer protects my agency. Prayer becomes the simple
> every day work that we do which allows God to grant
> the blessings he is already willing to grant us but are
> conditional on our willingness to ask. I believe He
> respects my will so profoundly that He wants me to
> exercise it whenever possible. No one requires me to
> pour out my soul; no one requires me to ask for cer-
> tain blessings; no one insists that I kneel in reverence.
> Prayer becomes an expression of my agency.[37]

I believe there has never been a sincere petition to our Heavenly
Father that has not been answered. Our Heavenly Father answering
prayers is not a problem; instead, our problem is we are sometimes
hesitant to ask for the desires of our heart. President Kimball implores,
"If in . . . prayer we hold back from the Lord, it may mean that some
blessings may be withheld from us. After all, we pray as petitioners
before an all-wise Heavenly Father, so why should we ever think to
hold back feelings or thoughts which bear upon our needs and our
blessings?"[38]

Even an apostle of the Lord had to be reminded to ask for the desires of his heart. During Elder Neal A. Maxwell's battle with leukemia, his wife taught him about asking. Biographer Bruce C. Hafen explains:

> Elder Maxwell felt he had no claim to a special miracle. He would talk about such people as Richard L. Evans, Bruce R. McConkie, A. Theodore Tuttle, Marvin J. Ashton and other General Authorities who had met death early. They were better men than I am, he would say. He didn't want to give any false hopes, and as one friend put it, he didn't want "to promote a fan club to demand a miracle."
>
> . . . And if it was time to face death, he had no need to argue or, for him, much worse, to shrink from drinking whatever bitter cup was his.
>
> [His wife] Colleen saw things differently, and she didn't hesitate to coach him with the loving directness she had long cultivated. She could see that in his desire to accept what he had been allotted to him, he was reluctant to importune the Lord with much pleading. But she pointed out that Jesus' first cry in the Garden of Gethsemane was "If it be possible let this cup pass from me." Only after he had made this earnest plea did the Savior finally submit Himself with "Nevertheless not as I will, but as thou wilt" (Matthew 26:39). With Jesus as our example in all things, she said, it must be permissible to plead. Then of course we submit, as He did. [Elder Maxwell] saw her insight and agreed.[39]

Sister Maxwell's tutoring brought her husband and the Church several additional years as the Lord blessed them in prayer. As Colleen Maxwell taught her husband, we are justified in voicing our desires to our Heavenly Father. Fervent prayer availeth much (James 5:16) as we are to call upon Him in *mighty* prayer (Enos 1:4, emphasis added). The Lord knows when we deeply desire something and are putting forth the necessary spiritual energy to have His blessings revealed. The Lord will answer us if we cry unto him for a long time with exceeding faith

(Ether 1:43). He honors persistence. The parable of the unjust judge demonstrates that persistence is expected and rewarded:

> There was in a city a judge, which feared not God, neither regarded man:
>
> And there was a widow in that city; and she came unto him, saying Avenge me of mine adversary.
>
> And he would not for a while: but afterward he said within himself, Though I fear not God, nor regard man;
>
> Yet because this widow troubleth me, I will avenge her, lest by her continual coming she weary me.
>
> And the Lord said, Hear what the unjust judge saith.
>
> And shall not God avenge his own elect, which cry day and night unto him, though he bear long with them?
>
> I tell you that he will avenge them speedily. (Luke 18: 2–8; see also D&C 101:82–84)

The Lord will speedily avenge His own elect that cry to Him day and night. He will also grant them their hearts' desires. The Lord wants us to continually come to Him, but unlike the unjust judge, He is never weary of our petitions. Unfortunately, most of us weary of our own petitions long before they are granted. We must persist until we have received the blessing from the Lord or until He tells us it's no longer His will that we seek a specific blessing. [40]

Step 4: Work Like Everything Depends on You

In addition to mighty prayer, in order to receive answers we must do whatever is in our power to bring to pass blessings in our lives. Elder Loren C. Dunn, President of the Quorum of the Seventy, defined: "Faith is the ability to do what we are prompted to do and when we are prompted to do it." [41] Doctrine and Covenants 123:17 tells us, "Let us cheerfully do all things that lie in our power; and then may we stand still, with the utmost assurance, to see the salvation of God, and for his arm to be revealed."

Work is involved in receiving answers to prayer. In Joseph Smith's history, the prophet provides examples of the kind of work needed. Joseph tells us he gave the matter of which church to join serious reflection and that his desires were deeply thought through (vs. 8). Joseph had worked to come to a decision and tells us he was partial to joining with the Methodists (vs. 8). Joseph had done his homework before approaching the Lord in the Sacred Grove. He tells us he went to church meetings and studied. In short, he did everything on his own that he could, including making a decision (vs. 9). Likewise, we might ask ourselves if we have gone as far as necessary to solve our own dilemmas as we can and if we are leaning toward some direction. Joseph also worked to find solutions by reading scripture (vs. 11). We would be wise to ask ourselves, "Have I gone to the scriptures for an answer?" I have found that in prayer the Lord lets us do all the talking while He listens. With scriptures, He talks while we listen. The Lord has given us the scriptures to help us find answers and solutions to our struggles. Searching the holy scriptures is part of the faith process.

Work usually precedes answers to prayers. For instance, one might ask in prayer, "Is the Book of Mormon true?" The Lord might respond by asking, "Will you read the book forever? Will you follow its precepts?" We might answer, "I don't know; tell me if it's true first." The Holy Ghost does not work that way. We have to do the work of reading the sacred volume first before we will be blessed with the witness of its truthfulness. We might also ask, "Is Gordon B. Hinckley a prophet?" The Lord may respond, "Will you will follow him?"[42] As President David O. McKay counsels, answers to prayers come as a natural sequence to the performance of duty.[43] Often the Lord will see if we will do whatever is in our power to bring a blessing in our lives before He will answer our prayers.

Sometimes we falter and make the mistake of expecting the Lord to do more than His part. Throughout scripture, it is evident that unless a person does all in his power, the arm of the Lord may not be revealed in his behalf. After one has truly sacrificed and done all in his power, God will come through and save him in his time of need. Sometimes the hardest work is to stand back after we have done our part and let the Lord work wonders. Such a stance is symbolically portrayed in the following story.

An acquaintance of mine told of growing up in Pima, Arizona. As a young boy he would go up in the mountains with his father and the ranch hands to check fences. This task took a few days, so they would prepare with overnight gear and supplies. On one particular trip, the boy's father picked a horse for him that would be gentle and not spook easily. His father felt this horse would be safe for his son to ride in the rough terrain. The horse had been owned by the boy's late grandfather and everyone called this horse the "old grey mare." It was a trustworthy horse in every way and everyone knew the young boy would be safe on it. Everything went as planned until the end of the first day out when the old grey mare threw a shoe. Horses without shoes in the mountains do not do well, and it became necessary to send the horse back with the boy. As he prepared to head home, the father told his son that if he would follow his instructions, he would have no problems finding his way. The boy was scared but he knew his Father would not mislead him. The father's instructions were as follows:

> Follow the fence line. If you will just stay close to the fence you will be safe and not lose your way. Remember when it gets dark you will have to ride closer to the fence, so don't lose sight of it. When you get closer to home, it will be dark and the ranch is not on the fence line. The old grey mare will know how to find the way home. As it gets dark, you will have to let go of the reins and trust. I promise you the old grey mare will take you safely home.

The boy knew his safety depended on following the instructions explicitly. As his father had said, darkness came, and the fence became harder to see. The boy had not been as close to the fence when it was light, but in the darkness, he had to not only stay close to the fence but also strain to see it. He became frightened, but he knew the old grey mare would be his ultimate safety. As he got closer and closer to home, it became darker and darker, until the boy could not see the fence at all. He was afraid but trusted his father and dropped the reins. The horse made a turn away from the invisible fence line, and before long the boy saw the lights of home in the distance. He had dropped the reins when he could no longer see and had been led safely back home.

If a young boy can place such trust in an old grey mare, we can surely have faith in the Savior of the world. We are all following a path, and the Lord knows the way back home. Our instructions are sometimes to simply trust him. Our fence line could be called the iron rod. When it becomes dark, we have to stay closer to the rod and sometimes strain at times to see it. When the time comes, and it always does in life, when you and I cannot see the future, we must sometimes drop the reigns and let the Lord take us to our destination. Sometimes the hardest thing to do is the work of trusting and doing nothing.

Step 5:
Prepare for Intense Trials

Once we try to increase our faith, it has been my experience that the adversary will get involved and the Ds will hit. No sooner do we begin to display a little faith then that faith will be tried. Though this natural phenomenon may seem unfair, without trials that even come to early faith, greater things cannot be revealed to us. [44] Moroni instructed, "I would show unto the world that faith is things which are hoped for and not seen: wherefore, dispute not because you see not, for ye receive no witness until after a trail of your faith" (Ether 12:6).

In our desire to increase our faith and receive answers to prayer we must prepare ourselves for intense trials. We might ask, "How do we prepare for intense trials?" Do we just grit our teeth? No! Instead, right up front, we can make a promise like this one: "Heavenly Father, if for some reason this does not work out, I will not get mad. I will keep my testimony intact and I will continue to petition until thou tells me to quit."

Martha in the New Testament gives us an example of this kind of attitude when she loses her brother Lazarus. You will remember that Martha's brother Lazarus is extremely ill when they send for Jesus to come help, but he does not come (John 11:6). Can you imagine having your brother, son, or husband in the hospital and calling for the home teachers or the bishop to come give your loved one a blessing, but they do not come, and your loved one dies before a priesthood blessing can be given? Can you see the mind set Martha might have had? I love Martha because she gives us a pattern of how to prepare for intense trials. When Martha hears that Christ is coming down the road her reaction is to run to him. "Then Martha as soon as she heard that Jesus was coming went and met him; but Mary sat still in the house" (John 11:20). The Lord does not expect us to be Pollyannas. When a trial is hard, it is okay to say so, and it is appropriate to say to the Lord in prayer, "This is difficult." Martha explains her feelings when she states, "Lord, if thou hadst been here, my brother had not died" (John 11:21). Even though things had not gone the way Martha wanted, she still keeps her testimony intact. That is a key to preparing for trials: we can decide not to curse God and to keep our testimonies intact. Martha does this as she bears her testimony to Jesus. She states,

> But I know, that even now, whatsoever thou wilt ask of God, God will give it thee. . . . Martha saith unto him, I know that he shall rise again in the resurrection at the last day. Jesus said unto her, I am the resurrection, and the life: he that believeth in me, though he were dead, yet shall he live: And whosoever liveth and believeth in me shall never die. Believest thou this? She saith unto him, Yea, Lord: I believe that thou art the Christ, the son of God, which should come into the world. And when she had so said, she went her way, and called Mary her sister secretly. (John 11:22, 24–28)

Once we start to petition the Lord for a blessing, there will be opposition. No sooner do we begin to display a little faith then that faith will be tried. Without trials, which come even to early faith, greater things cannot be revealed to us. Joseph Smith experienced this in the Sacred Grove as he tried to pray.

> But, exerting all my powers to call upon God to deliver me out of the power of this enemy which had seized upon me, and at the very moment when I was ready to sink into despair and abandon myself to destruction—not to an imaginary ruin, but to the power of some actual being from the unseen world, who had such marvelous power as I had never before felt in any being—just at this moment of great alarm, I saw a pillar of light exactly over my head, above the brightness of the sun which descended gradually until it fell upon me (JS—H 1:16).

Joseph says relief did not come until the "moment of great alarm" (vs. 16). With us too the Lord may bring us to a moment of great alarm. He has a tendency to push us to our limit. When we feel that God has forsaken or forgotten us, if we endure He will bring down greater power. Sometimes he cannot intervene until we have hit our moment of great alarm because answers do come at a price. Intense trials such as those that Martha and Joseph Smith experienced and that we will experience will come especially when we are trying to accomplish good. Elder Jeffrey R. Holland explains:

> God takes us to the grove or the mountain or the temple and there shows us the wonder of what his plan was for us . . . The adversary and his pinched, calculating little minions try to oppose such experiences and then try to darken them after the fact. But that is not the way of the gospel. That is not the way of a Latter-day Saint who claims as the fundamental fact of the Restoration the spirit of revelation. Fighting through darkness and despair and pleading for the light is what opened this dispensation. It is what keeps it going, and it is what will keep you going. With Paul, I say to all of you, "Cast not away therefore your confidence, which hath great recompense of reward. For if ye have need of patience, that after ye have done the will of God ye might receive the promise" (Hebrews 10:35–36) . . . "Fear ye not . . . The Lord shall fight for you." [45]

As we prepare for and go through intense trials the Lord will fight for us and bless our efforts as we exercise faith and expect Him to intervene.

Step 6:
Expect the Lord to Intervene in Your Behalf

Expectation must be part of the faith equation. There is a wonderful story in 2 Kings 3 about the children of Israel who show us this pattern as they experience a drought. In the scriptures King Jehoshaphat calls for the prophet Elisha to solve the drought problem. Elisha commands the king to "make this valley full of ditches" (vs. 16). Then the Lord promises, "Ye shall not see any wind, neither shall ye see rain; yet that valley shall be filled with water" (vs. 17). We might ask figuratively, "What ditches do I need to dig to show the Lord I have faith in his intervening?" The Lord will tell us what to do in such situations. President McKay said, "When the Lord tells you what to do, you have to have the courage to do what he instructs you." [46] "You've got to desire [an answer] with all your soul! You've got to have all the intensity of which you are capable and a desire that this is the most prized thing in all the world for which you seek!" [47] Elder Cook suggests, "When you start praying, you've got to believe as if your request has already been granted." We too can pray with expectation, as if our righteous desires have come to pass. We can go to the Lord and say, "According to my best understanding this is what I feel will happen," and we can expect the Lord to intervene. [48] Elder Cook explains,

> I believe that many people are confident that the Lord's will be done and that the Lord can do anything, but they're not confident that he will do it for them or that he wants to do it now. This lack of confidence in our ability to gain access to the power of heaven is a major reason why more of our prayers aren't answered. . . . I often meet people who say, My prayer wasn't answered because it just wasn't the will of the Lord." They want to place the responsibility for their unanswered prayer on the Lord. But often the truth is that they just didn't exercise enough faith; they didn't have enough confidence in their ability to receive an answer. [49]

Nothing is too hard for the Lord (Genesis 18:14). Elder John H. Groberg of the Quorum of the Seventy promises,

> If we pray with all of our heart for that which is right, that which is according to God's will, it will be granted as the scriptures promise. The key, of course, is to be willing to accept His will and ask only for those things that are according to His will. In fact, I don't believe you can pray in faith except for those things that are according to His will. [50]

If our faith has increased while praying for something, we can know we are on the right track. Elder Groberg found that the Tongan Saints he lived with understood this principle. When he was a district president, a government telegram arrived, demanding that Elder Groberg close a Church school. His counselors suggested, "Let's call a special fast before we tell members, as they have sacrificed so much. We feel it would be better if we didn't close down. We think the Lord will see it our way, but we have to get through to Him first." When another telegram arrived which said the decision to close the school had been reversed, Elder Groberg ran to his counselors to tell them the good news. His counselors showed little excitement and simply nodded knowingly, with a sort of "what-else-do-you-expect? attitude."[51] When we ask in faith, we can expect the Lord's intervention also.

The Bible Dictionary explains that "faith is a principle of action and of power, and by it one can command the elements and/or heal the sick, or influence any number of circumstances when occasion warrants."[52] Faith can invite the powers of heaven. In the end it will not be our influence that will directly change and influence other's lives, rather the influence of our faith will invite the influence of heaven, and God will then change lives and hearts.

While displaying faith we must have an absolute expectation that answers to our prayers will come forth. Some people say "I'll try it but I'm sure it won't work" and they are right. Others say, "I don't know how this will work, but the Lord has promised, and I have confidence it will" and they are right—they are exercising faith.[53] When we begin to question our ability to receive answers to prayers, it may be helpful to send a flash prayer to heaven saying, "Lord, I believe; help thou my unbelief" (Mark 9:24).

Answers to Prayer

The Lord will answer our prayers in four general ways:

One answer is yes. We will see our hearts' desire develop and experience great love for our Heavenly Father's blessings in our lives. We will feel great joy when we receive a yes.

Another answer is no. Receiving a no is different than not receiving an answer. If we get a no answer from the Lord, we will have a tremendous feeling of peace accompanying that answer. These are two feelings that Satan cannot duplicate—peace and joy. And these two feelings are accompanied by yes and no answers.

A third type of answer is yes, but with variations. Examples of such an answer might include: "Yes, I want you to move, but not in that neighborhood." "Yes, you'll get to go to law school, but not at BYU." One "yes, but with variations" for me was "Yes, you'll teach religion, but not in the seminary program."

The final type of answer is "Yes, but later!" This is the hardest of all answers to receive because we then have to keep importuning. Elder Gene R. Cook explains how we can deal with a "yes, but later" answer to our prayers:

> When we pray for something that does not occur the way we desire it to, we must not lose faith. In the Lord's own way and time all righteous prayers are answered but His way and His time may not be the same as ours. Sometimes when a prayer appears to go unanswered, it is because it is being answered in a greater way than we can perceive. When we face these trials, we must double our faith lest we lose it. [54]

At one time in Joseph Smith's life, he received a "yes, but later" answer to prayer. When Joseph was visited by Angel Moroni on September 22, 1824 (according to his mother), Joseph was told he could try to obtain the plates and the whole family anxiously anticipated Joseph receiving them. Joseph described prying a stone that covered the plates and putting forth his hand, and then lifting them from their place. According to his mother,

> In the excitement of the moment, he laid the record down in order to cover up the box . . . When he turned again to take up the record, it was gone, but where he knew not, nor did he know by what means it had been taken away. He was much alarmed at this. He knelt down and asked the Lord why it was that the record was taken from him. The angel appeared to him and told him that he had not done as he was commanded, for in a former revelation he had been commanded not to lay the plates down, or put them

for a moment out of his hands . . . After some further conversation, Joseph was permitted to raise the
stone again, and there he beheld the plates, the same
as before. He reached forth his hand to take them, but
was hurled to the ground with great violence. When
he recovered, the angel was gone, and he arose and
returned to the house, weeping for grief and disappointment. [55]

Joseph was concerned that his family would doubt him when he
returned home plateless. When he related his experience, his parents
believed him but began to fear that he might never qualify to obtain
the plates. The Smiths' support of their third-born son must have
brought great solace to this future prophet, for when Joseph seemed
not to be making progress with the Angel Moroni, Lucy tells us
they "doubled [their] diligence in prayer and supplication to God." [56]
Keeping our faith strong and vibrant during such times is vital to our
receiving answers.

Elder Richard G. Scott adds this counsel:

Our Heavenly Father did not put us on earth to fail
but to succeed gloriously. It may seem paradoxical,
but that is why recognizing answers to prayer can
sometimes be very difficult. Some face life with only
their own experience and capacity to help them.
Others seek, through prayer, divine inspiration to
know what to do. When it is required, they qualify for
power beyond their own capacity to do it.

Communication with our Father in Heaven is not a
trivial matter. It is a sacred privilege. It is based on
unchanging principles. When we receive help from
our Father in Heaven, it is in response to faith, obedience, and the purposes of agency.

It is a mistake to assume that every prayer we offer
will be answered immediately. Some prayers require
considerable effort on our part. True, sometimes
impressions come when we have not specifically sought
them. They generally concern something we need to
know and are not otherwise able to find out. [57]

With faith we can remember that "God's delays are not God's denials." [58] Our Father in Heaven is anxious to bless us. Elder Maxwell explains further:

> In modern revelation we are told very frankly . . . that "when we obtain any blessings from God it is by obedience to that law upon which it is predicated" (D&C 130:21). I don't know how it is for you, but I have felt so often in my life so greatly blessed for what little obedience I have given. My conclusion with regard to that verse is that the Lord's ratio of blessings to our obedience is a very generous ratio indeed. He is so quick to reward us, so quick to reassure us, and so anxious to take delight when we serve him. So if you puzzle over that verse, as I have in my life, including in recent times, the only bottom line I can give you is that the ratio of blessings to our miniscule obedience is a very, very generous ratio indeed. . . .
>
> Have I had some prayers that were not answered? Yes, and so have you. Sometimes the reason is that we may ask for something without enough faith, or we may in fact ask for something that isn't expedient or that isn't right. For us to get used to the fact that all prayers are not automatically answered is one of life's growing experiences.
>
> Some prayers are answered dramatically . . . With others we must importune and wait. But if we do that, there will come to us in those waiting moments special things. [59]

If the answer we receive in prayer is "yes, but later" as explained above, we must continue to importune during those waiting moments. If circumstances or suffering go unrelieved, we may quit importuning the Lord too soon. In the past, maybe if we had importuned a little longer, things might be different. We might ask, " 'How can we balance sincere importuning with submissively accepting what God has allotted to us?' Only the Holy Ghost can give us such discernment and assurance." [60] The Spirit will tell us when our importuning has been sufficient and when it is time to accept what is allotted because we will feel peaceful about discontinuing our efforts.

The Lord is ever anxious to intervene in our lives as we develop and use faith. The most repeated promise in the standard works is "Ask, and it shall be given you; seek, and ye shall find; knock, and it shall be opened unto you" (Matthew 7:7). Truly, the Lord has rewarded those who exercise faith in the past. In Hebrews 11, Paul reminds us of times when faith brought blessings. Paul's list includes: Abel offering sacrifice, Noah building the Ark, Abraham receiving his lands of inheritance and offering Isaac, Sarah having Isaac, Isaac blessing Jacob, Jacob blessing Joseph, Moses being saved as a baby and passing through the Red Sea with the children of Israel, the walls of Jericho coming down, and the harlot Rahab being saved.

In Ether 12, Moroni has his own list of the rewarders of faith: Christ showed himself to the Americans, Alma and Amulek were released from prison, Ammon converted the Lamanites, the three disciples were translated, and the brother of Jared saw Christ (Ether 12:7–19).

Each of us might have our own faith list as we experience answers to prayer and increase faith. I have my own faith list that includes the following: by faith Mary Jane Woodger was able to finish a doctorate when she could not get accepted to a Master's program; by faith Mary Jane Woodger was able to teach at Brigham Young University when she was rejected for teaching seminary. My list continues to grow as I exercise faith in the Lord Jesus Christ. Someday, I will say by faith Mary Jane Woodger found her companion and bore children either here or there.

My students at Brigham Young University have also exercised faith and accomplished incredible things. By faith, one who wanted to marry met her husband. By faith one whose sister ran away from home returned home for Christmas. And by faith one who wanted to share the Gospel was able to with a friend. What does your personal list of faith accomplishments include? Faith is the essence of the Gospel and the essence of self-esteem. Faith is one of the attributes of our Savior and our Heavenly Father. If when we see Him we are truly going to be like him, we must also possess faith.

1. Neal A. Maxwell, *Lord, Increase Our Faith* (Salt Lake City: Deseret Book, 1994), 41.

2. Joseph Smith, comp., *Lectures on Faith* (Salt Lake City: Deseret Book, 1985), 71.

3. Jeffrey R. Holland, "Cast Not Away Therefore Your Confidence," *Brigham Young University 1998–99 Speeches* (Provo: Brigham Young University Publications and Graphics, 1999), 156, 160.

4. *Church News*, 29 April 1984, 5.

5. Lavina Fielding Anderson, "Dallin H. Oaks: The Disciplined Edge," *Ensign*, April 1981, 37.

6. Gene R. Cook, "Faith in the Lord Jesus Christ," Brigham Young University Fireside, 8 November 1981, 38–39.

7. Joseph Smith, comp., *Lectures on Faith* (Salt Lake City: Deseret Book, 1985), 3.

8. Ibid., 24.

9. Boyd K. Packer, "What is Faith?" in *Faith* (Salt Lake City: Deseret Book, 1983), 42–43.

10. Gene R. Cook, *Receiving Answers to Our Prayers* (Salt Lake City: Deseret Book, 1996), 42–43.

11. Neal A. Maxwell, *Lord, Increase Our Faith* (Salt Lake City: Bookcraft, 1994), 2.

12. Joseph Smith, comp., *Lectures on Faith* (Salt Lake City: Deseret Book, 1985), 41.

13. Ibid.

14. Gene R. Cook, *Receiving Answers to Our Prayers* (Salt Lake City: Deseret Book, 1996), 122.

15. Neal A. Maxwell, *Lord, Increase Our Faith* (Salt Lake City: Bookcraft, 1994), 38.

16. Robert C. Oaks, "Understand Who You Are." Brigham Young University Devotional, 21 March 2006, 1.

17. Joseph Smith, comp., *Lectures on Faith* (Salt Lake City: Deseret Book, 1985), 41.

18. Henry B. Eyring, "We Must Raise Our Sights," *The Religious Educator* (Provo: BYU Religious Studies Center, 2001) vol. 2, no. 2, 10 (emphasis added).

19. Joseph Smith, comp., *Lectures on Faith* (Salt Lake City: Deseret Book, 1985), 41.

20. William Clayton, "The Historians Corner," *BYU Studies* vol. 18, no. 3, Spring 1978, 477.

21. Naomi Randall, "I am a Child of God," *Hymns of The Church of Jesus Christ of Latter-day Saints* (Salt Lake City: The Church of Jesus Christ of Latter-day Saints, 1985), 301.

22. Virginia H. Pearce, Unpublished email of notes on "Prayer," Tri-Ward Fireside, 20 January 2002. In possession of Mary Jane Woodger.

23. David O. McKay, *Conference Report*, April 1964, 115.

24. Joseph Smith, comp., *Lectures on Faith* (Salt Lake City: Deseret Book, 1985), 38.

25. Spencer W. Kimball, *Teachings of Spencer W. Kimball,* ed. Edward L. Kimball (Salt Lake City: Bookcraft, 1982), 451.

26. Neal A. Maxwell, "The Christ-Centered Life," *Ensign*, August 1981, 13.

27. Gene R. Cook, *Receiving Answers to Our Prayers* (Salt Lake City: Deseret Book, 1996), 2.

28. Dean C. Jesse, "The Early Accounts of Joseph Smith's First Vision [1831–1839]," *BYU Studies* vol. 9, no. 3, Spring 1969, 279.

29. James E. Faust, "Trying to Serve the Lord Without Offending the Devil," Brigham Young University Devotional, 15 November 1994, 1.

30. Gene R. Cook, *Receiving Answers to Our Prayers* (Salt Lake City: Deseret Book, 1996), 25.

31. Harold B. Lee, *Stand Ye in Holy Places* (Salt Lake City: Deseret Book, 1974), 244.

32. Gordon B. Hinckley, *Teachings of Gordon B. Hinckley* (Salt Lake City: Bookcraft, 1997), 469.

33. Spencer W. Kimball, "Prayer," *New Era*, March 1978, 15–16.

34. Gene R. Cook, *Receiving Answers to Our Prayers* (Salt Lake City: Deseret Book, 1996), 139.

35. Spencer W. Kimball, "Prayer," *New Era*, March 1978, 15–16.

36. The Holy Bible: Authorized Version with Explanatory Notes and Cross References to the Standard Works of The Church of Jesus Christ of Latter-day Saints, (Salt Lake City: The Church of Jesus Christ of Latter-day Saints, 1986), 752–753.

37. Virginia H. Pearce, Unpublished email notes on "Prayer," Tri-Ward Fireside, 20 January 2002. In possession of Mary Jane Woodger.

38. Spencer W. Kimball, *Teachings of Spencer W. Kimball*, ed. Edward L. Kimball (Salt Lake City: Bookcraft, 1982), 125.

39. Bruce C. Hafen, *A Disciple's Life: The Biography of Neal A. Maxwell* (Salt Lake City, Deseret Book, 2002), 14–15.

40. Gene R. Cook, *Receiving Answers to Our Prayers* (Salt Lake City: Deseret Book, 1996), 154.

41. Loren C. Dunn, "Building Bridges to Faith" in *Faith* (Salt Lake City: Deseret Book, 1983), 81.

42. Unpublished notes, S. Michael Wilcox, Education Week, 1999.

43. David O. McKay, *The Teachings of David O. McKay*, comp. Mary Jane Woodger (Salt Lake City: Deseret Book, 2004), 237.

44. Jeffrey R. Holland, "Cast Not Away Therefore Your Confidence," *Brigham Young University 1998–1999 Speeches* (Provo: Brigham Young University Publications and Graphics, 1999), 156.

45. Ibid., 160–161.

46. Harold B. Lee quoting President David O. McKay, *Conference Report*, October 1962, 82.

47. Harold B. Lee, *Teachings of Harold B. Lee*, ed. Clyde W. Williams (Salt Lake City: Deseret Book, 2001), 125.

48. Gene R. Cook, *Receiving Answers to Our Prayers* (Salt Lake City: Deseret Book, 1996), 152 and 62–63.

49. Ibid., 60.

50. John H. Groberg, *The Other Side of Heaven* (Salt Lake City: Bookcraft, 1993), 102.

51. Ibid., 166.

52. *The Holy Bible: Authorized Version with Explanatory Notes and Cross References to the Standard Works of The Church of Jesus Christ of Latter-day Saints*, (Salt Lake City: The Church of Jesus Christ of Latter-day Saints, 1986), 670.

53. Gene R. Cook, *Receiving Answers to Our Prayers* (Salt Lake City: Deseret Book, 1996), 55–56.

54. Gene R. Cook, "Faith in the Lord Jesus Christ" in *Faith* (Salt Lake City: Deseret Book, 1983), 102.

55. Lucy Mack Smith, *The Revised and Enhanced History of Joseph Smith by his Mother*, Eds. Scot Facer Proctor and Maurine Jensen Proctor (Salt Lake City: Bookcraft, 1996), 122–123. See Joseph Knight's account of the 1824 meeting in Dean C. Jesse, ed., "Joseph Knight's recollection of Early Mormon History," *BYU Studies* vol. 17, no 1, Autumn 1976, 122–123.

56. Ibid., 124.

57. Richard G. Scott, "Learning to Recognize Answers to Prayer," *Ensign*, November 1989, 30.

58. Robert Harold Schueller, *Tough Times Never Last, But Tough People Do!* (New York: Bantam Books, 1983), 87.

59. Neal A. Maxwell, "Sharing Insights from My life," *Brigham Young University 1998–99 Speeches* (Provo: Brigham Young University Publications and Graphics, 1999), 111, 116.

60. Neal A. Maxwell, *Lord, Increase Our Faith* (Salt Lake City: Bookcraft, 1994), 37.

Chapter 4
Being as *Abraham*

I CANNOT JUST HOPE FOR ETERNAL LIFE, although that is my ultimate hope. I also hope things will get better in this life and that blessings really are predicated upon keeping laws. I must have faith in what our Heavenly Father says in Doctrine and Covenants 130:20–21: "There is a law irrevocably decreed in heaven before the foundation of this world, upon which all blessings are predicated and when we obtain any blessing from God it is by obedience to that law upon which it is predicated." Learn the law, live the law, reap the blessing.

As a single Latter-day Saint woman, I have held on to promises given me in respect to marriage, family, and a companion. Those promises have been given in the form of priesthood blessings, a patriarchal blessing, a father's blessing, bishop's blessings, and a stake president's blessing. I have clung to the words in those blessings that have promised I will not always be alone.

Today, I can look back and thank my Heavenly Father for not always answering my prayers the way I wanted. Now that my heart has healed from several failed relationships, I can honestly thank my Heavenly Father that they married someone else. Each relationship and prospective spouse got better, and I am sure whoever I end up with will be more than I expected. Then promises from a stake president who told me my husband would be worth the wait, and a patriarch who promised me one that would be worthy, eligible, and prepared will be realized. Such words have been beacons to me and have eased the pain of broken hearts, lonely moments, and as of now unfulfilled dreams.

However, there was a time when these promises seemed obliterated, and the Lord's promises were temporarily taken away. During this time I felt I went through an Abrahamic test. I define an Abrahamic test as the Lord giving you something, and then it seems He takes it away. Job went through such a test, and it was he who coined an important concept. Although Job was told by his friends to curse God, he continued to be faithful. That is what an Abrahamic test is really all about. We are tempted to quit believing and expecting that our Heavenly Father will keep his promises. You will remember that Job simply said as he was undergoing his test, "The Lord gave, and the Lord hath taken away; blessed be the name of the Lord" (Job 1:21). I would suggest that if you feel the Lord has given you something after a test of faith and then has taken it away, you are going through an Abrahamic test.

Our tests are certainly not as harsh as the Lord asking that we sacrifice an only son; nevertheless, when the Lord is testing you in the most tender, sensitive, important areas of your emotions and life, He is testing you as he tested Abraham. He is testing you for Godhood. Those who still struggle with paying their tithing, going to church, or keeping morally clean are not usually experiencing Abrahamic tests and sometimes it seems the better you are, the more severe the test we may experience.

Elder A. Theodore Tuttle of the First Quorum of the Seventy who died after several months' suffering with cancer in November 1986 said:

> At times it seems that even God is punishing us and ours. One of the things that makes all this so hard to bear is that we ourselves appear to be chosen for this affliction while others presumably escape these adversities. . . . [But] we cannot indulge ourselves the luxury of self-pity. [1]

Abraham and Job were certainly two of Heavenly Father's most noble children. In Abraham's story (and I might add his wife Sarah's story also, whose part in this test is veiled), you never catch a whiff of self-pity, only hope. President John Taylor in speaking of Abraham tells us of Joseph Smith's commentary about this ancient father:

Joseph Smith, who, when speaking of these things, said God was determined in these days to have a tried people as he had in former times, and that he would feel after their heartstrings and try them in every way possible for them to be tried; and if he could have invented anything that would have been more keen, acute, and trying than that which he required of Abraham he would have done it. [2]

The Lord tested Abraham in the most sensitive of areas. It may be hard for you and I to think of a loving Heavenly Father who would design a trial that is keen, acute, and heart-wrenching. Such actions hardly seem to equate love; however paradoxically acute, heart wrenching trials are very much part of a loving Heavenly Father's tutoring of his favored children. Abraham was one such favored child.

Abraham grew up in a difficult situation. His father, Terah, wavered back and forth between idolatry and keeping the Lord's commandments. Abraham never knew what to expect from his father. It would have been better if Terah would have been a consistent idolater. Such "wishy-washy" upbringing can create emotional scars. The epitome of Terah's wickedness was when Terah wanted to sacrifice his son. Speaking of this dangerous situation, Abraham simply records, "I, Abraham, saw that it was needful for me to obtain another place of residence" (Abraham 1:1). I have always thought this was the epitome of understatement. Circumstances precipitating this potential sacrifice show us that Abraham had a courageous personality. John Taylor describes Abraham's actions preceding his father's attempted sacrifice as follows:

> Abraham's father had instructed him in the doctrines of these idols, and had sought to induce him to have faith in them and in their power, authority, and dominion, telling him what great personages they were.

> But Abraham, inspired by the Lord, went on a certain occasion into the temple of these gods and smote them right and left, upsetting and breaking them in pieces. His father came in and asked what he had been doing, what great sin this was that he had committed, why he was so sacrilegious in his feelings and so wicked as to seek to destroy these gods?

Said he, "Father, I did not do anything to them, they quarreled among themselves and went to work fighting and knocked one another down, broke one another's heads and knocked off one another's arms and legs."

"Oh," said his father, "my son do not tell me anything of that kind, for they are made of wood and they could not move or stir from their place nor knock one another down; it has been some other agency that has done it."

"Why, father," said he, "would you worship a being that could not stir or move, that had hands and could not handle, that had legs and could not walk, a mouth that could not speak, and a head and it was of no use? Would you worship a being like that?" But nevertheless our history informs us that the priests were angry and stirred up his father against him. [3]

The result of his father being "stirred up against him" was Abraham being placed on an altar to be sacrificed.

After being saved by an angel, Abraham is told by the Lord to go into the wilderness, leaving all he had known. Ironically, even with growing up with that kind of father, Abraham's fondest desire is to become a father himself. That is his greatest hope. I am sure he hoped for Eternal Life, but Abraham also had a hope for his mortal life. He had a hope that his righteous desire would be fulfilled in mortality. Abraham knew there is greater happiness, peace, and rest in family life; he wanted those blessings in mortality and sought for them. In Abraham 1:2–3 this greatest of patriarchs reveals,

And, finding there was greater happiness and peace and rest for me, I sought for the blessings of the fathers, and the right whereunto I should be ordained to administer the same; having been myself a follower of righteousness, desiring also to be one who possessed great knowledge, and to be a greater follower of righteousness, and to possess a greater knowledge, and to be a father of many nations, a prince of peace, and desiring to receive instructions, and to keep the commandments of God, I became a rightful heir, a

High Priest, holding the right belonging to fathers. It
was conferred on me from the fathers; it came down
from the fathers (Abraham 1:2–3).

Notice in the verses above how often Abraham repeats the word
father. Abraham had an obsession: he wanted to be a father. That was
the most important thing to him and he wrote and spoke of it as a possibility. Here is this incredibly righteous person, who can call down
an angel to save him, who, when the Lord says, "Get thee out . . .
from thy father's house," "he went out, not knowing whither he went"
(Genesis 12:1 and Hebrews 11:8). He is "true blue" valiant, and there
is only one blessing he really wants. He just wants to have a family life.
Then he goes through long years of childlessness with his wife Sarah.
Paul tells us that during those years Abraham laid his hands on Sarah's
head and promised her she would conceive, and she believed him.
Sarah also had a hope. She absolutely expected to become a mother and
then went through years without a pregnancy (Hebrews 11:11).

Then Abraham is finally blessed with a son, Ishmael. I am not sure
circumstances of that birth are exactly what Abraham had envisioned.
Then what happens? The Lord tells Abraham to send Ishmael away.
Ishmael almost dies and the Lord reassures Abraham that it will be
okay! Abraham must have been a bit perplexed. The trial of not being
a father is not a one-time experience or a one-sided thing. The Lord's
test comes at Abraham in every possible manner.

Then miracle of miracles, he and Sarah have Isaac and raise him.
Isaac seems to be every parent's dream as he grows, develops, and
becomes an adult. We know that Isaac was not a young boy at the time
of his almost sacrifice. He was a grown man; scholars put him symbolically at around the age of thirty-three.[4] Here was the son who would
carry the promise to bring many nations to Abraham, and what does
the Lord do? It seems He takes the promise away. The Lord giveth
(and we would say it takes him a long time to give in this case), and
now Abraham must have thought, "He is taking it away." John Taylor
related Abraham's experience in this way:

> He saw in this, apparently, all his hopes blasted; but
> notwithstanding he had faith and confidence in God,
> and he stood there like the beaten anvil to the stroke,
> or the sturdy oak defying all storms and blasts and
> influences. He was strong in faith, giving glory to

God. Nothing but the spirit of revelation could have given him this confidence, and it was that which sustained him under these peculiar circumstances. [5]

Amazingly, the scriptures tell us Abraham did not wait to make his decision about the Lord's request. He got up early in the morning; he did not even sleep in on that fateful day (Genesis 22:3–4). The Lord was taking away the very promise He had given, but Abraham kept trusting the Lord, even when his deepest heartstrings were being pulled. Abraham must have felt like his aorta was being severed.

We can imagine this patriarch thinking, "This is strange. The Lord is asking me to do the same thing my father did that made me leave my home. Well if I have to do this, if this is a personal commandment the Lord is giving me, though it makes no sense at all, I'll do it." I can imagine Abraham's irony, "I never wanted to be like my father. Here I am repeating his worst sin, and I am told by the Lord it is the right thing to do." Paul tells us about Abraham's thoughts as follows:

> When he was tried, offered up Isaac: and he that had received the promises offered up his only begotten son, Of whom it was said, That in Isaac shall thy seed be called: Accounting that God *was* able to raise him up, even from the dead; from whence also he received him in a figure. (Hebrews 11:17–19)

In other words, Abraham believed, "If I am required to sacrifice my son, then I will kill him. But then I will lay my hands on his head and raise him from the dead." That was the hope of Abraham. He had the expectation the Lord would somehow keep His promises and He did, but not in the way Abraham envisioned. Instead, the Lord provided a ram in the thicket. I would suggest that with hope, there will always be a ram for each of us, even when our heartstrings are being wrenched. This is one of the great lessons the Lord gives in the story of Abraham almost sacrificing Isaac, that the Lord truly does provide.

Our heartstrings are connected to our emotional experiences, something I learned firsthand through one of my own Abrahamic tests. I had met someone and at first did not like him at all. The first time he called to ask me on a date, he had the audacity to ask me questions to see if I measured up to spending an evening with him. I had to be within the right age range, never been married, have no children, listen to the right radio station, and even prefer Mexican over Chinese food. Luckily, or unluckily, I answered the questions correctly. I was a little amazed myself that I went out with him, but I had decided I would give anybody a chance who had the courage to ask me out. This man's opening quiz was almost more than I could handle, and it made for some delightful conversation among my friends.

During the first date, I remember looking across the car at this man, and thinking, "You look like a big clown face. I do not want to date a big clown face, so I am not going to go out with you again." But I did. After the second date I became very determined not to date the clown anymore, and I was contemplating how to let him down easy. However, through a series of spiritual events, including one in the temple and a setting apart by my bishop for a calling, the Lord revealed to me in the plainest way He has ever given that I was not to quit dating this man. Instead the Lord told me this man would make me happy. I was told in the setting apart that this relationship would progress, and I would begin a new phase of my life with this man.

I knew the promptings I was receiving were from the Lord because I changed my mind about seeing someone else I was dating. As I chose this course, one of my dearest friends stated she had never seen me change my mind after I had decided I was not interested in a man; she was right. My reactions and reversed attitude towards this man were uncharacteristic. When I decided to follow those promptings and allowed myself to be pursued by this man, I became emotionally attached very fast and saw him as part of my future. I could even see myself giving birth to little clown faces.

For the first time in my life I was having a courtship experience, and, more important, I had incredible feelings of joy and peace. I did not even flirt with this man. He was just there. He did everything right and said all the right things as the relationship moved forward quickly. When I was with him, I felt I was being led, guided, and even told what to say by the Spirit. People said I had a glow about me they had never seen before. It was like I had always imagined courtship would be. Before I knew it, we were talking about marriage. Then on the weekend that I was suppose to meet his parents, he dumped me in a cowardly way on my answering machine. From what I gathered, some of the reasons for terminating our relationship were that he thought I was coy and that he did not believe the Lord guided lives and I did. He felt he had an intelligent mind and the Lord expected him to use it.

He felt I was too reliant on the Lord. He was convinced the Lord did not really care where he worked, who he married, where he lived, and in short, was not in the details of our lives. Because I believed we can be led by the Spirit, he said good-bye. Immediately, he moved away to another city to start a career. I cried bucketfuls, but at the same time felt our relationship was not over and continued to have feelings of incredible peace as I continued to pray and fast in this man's behalf.

After eighteen months without any contact, this man called me on the phone and repeated to me some of the exact words I had fervently repeated in my prayers. This man had lost a loved one and said that during the experience my voice had gone through his mind over and over again. He then said words I had ached to hear: "You were right and I was wrong. The Lord really is involved in our lives and I am moving back to Salt Lake." Yet, after all of that, he married someone else, leaving me heartbroken and perplexed. Without the spiritual witnesses, I would have ended the relationship before getting my heart involved. At the time I said to the Lord, "I'm not getting this. This trial is where I am the most vulnerable. Thou knowest that." Did I curse the Lord? I did not this time. In previous, similar situations I had been pretty upset with the Lord, but this time I repented and tried to follow an Abrahamic attitude, the same stance Paul took where he states: "We are troubled on every side, yet not distressed; we are perplexed, but not in despair; Persecuted, but not forsaken; cast down, but not destroyed" (2 Corinthians 4:8).

I was perplexed, troubled, and cast down, but I was going to put my trust in the Lord and not be distressed, in despair, or destroyed by the experience. I wanted to be like Abraham, "the sturdy oak defying all storms and blasts." I wanted to be confident amidst some peculiar circumstances. I was in a quandary the night I talked with him on the phone as he gloated over the fact that he was marrying someone else. I did what I sometimes do when I have done everything I can do for my own emotional health, and peace will not come—I went for comfort from a priesthood blessing.

However, in choosing someone to give me a blessing, I went to a man I had never met. I made a mistake receiving a blessing from someone who did not have stewardship over me, yet he was a priesthood bearer. Looking back, I do not know if this priesthood bearer was not in tune or telling me what he wanted to instead of what the Lord had in mind. What I do know is that previously the Priesthood has always brought rest and peace, but this blessing brought despair, discord and confusion.

I spoke with this man before he gave me the blessing, telling him of my situation. As I shared my thoughts, he discounted every spiritual experience I had. He told me those experiences had been my emotions speaking. As I brought up blessings and promises I had previously received, he told me that the promises were from men telling me what I wanted to hear, making null and void all the promises most dear to my heart I had received. Before giving me the blessing, he told me to be prepared to hear some hard things.

The blessing itself was disheartening; I think I was in shock. I was told I would spend mortality alone, that no one was waiting in the wings for me, that my Heavenly Father was not preparing anyone for me, and it was too late for my hopes and dreams. The rest of the blessing was equally unpleasant. To say amen was difficult. When I went home, I had the most restless night of my life. The next Sunday I spoke with my bishop about the experience. My bishop told me that it was the first blessing of discomfort he had ever heard of and that the Lord does not give a stone when we ask for bread (Matthew 7:9).

Although I did not feel the Spirit during that blessing, at the same time it may have been an Abrahamic test from my Father in Heaven, especially crafted for me. Sometimes the Lord will give us a test and then he will say, "Not really, I have a greater blessing for you. I wanted you to learn if you would remain faithful." I am reminded of such a situation and the test he put Heber C. and Vilate Kimball through as well as John and Leonora Taylor.

The Prophet Joseph Smith came to both of these members of the Quorum of the Twelve and told them about plural marriage and then added a caveat: Vilate Kimball and Leonora Taylor were to be Joseph Smith's plural wives. Both couples went through torment as they tried to follow the prophet. I would suggest this was Leonora Taylor's greatest test. When John Taylor had asked Leonora Cannon for her hand in marriage, because she was twelve years older than him she basically told him to go find someone else his own age. Then Leonora had a dream wherein she was told by the Lord that John Taylor was to be her husband.[6] The Lord had given Leonora to John through that dream, and now He was taking her away. The story is told that Leonora got so angry before she submitted to the Lord's will that she put her hand through a window and severely cut her thumb. Her thumb then became infected and she lost it. Afterward, Leonora Taylor said every time she looked down at her thumbless hand she was reminded of the time she denied the prophet. Eventually Leonora, John, Heber, and Vilate all submitted to the will of our Heavenly Father. They were perplexed, but if Leonora and Vilate becoming Joseph's wives was what the Lord required, then so be it. Both couples went to Joseph Smith, and in essence John and Heber took their wives' hands, placed them in the hand of the prophet, and said she is yours. But there was a ram in the thicket. As they submitted to the Lord's will, Joseph told these two couples, "You have passed the test," and subsequently sealed them for time and all eternity. [7]

I am leery of comparing my situation with the experiences of the Kimballs' and Taylors', but my trial was severe and difficult for me. Eventually, I have renewed my hope in the Lord's promises. When I came to myself, I did not charge God foolishly for seeming to take away what I had been promised. I continue to hope, to expect, and to know the Lord keeps his promises despite a perplexing experience coming in the same way promises had come through priesthood blessings.

We can have faith that there will be a ram in the thicket—"but if not," we must be willing to trust that the Lord has something better planned for us (Daniel 3:18). Hope is expectation, but I would suggest it is even more than expecting. To have hope is acting as if something has already happened. It is an attitude within the perimeters of the gospel of Jesus Christ. Hope is for this life as well as the next. Yes, ultimately we hope for Eternal Life, but we can also hope that our lives, relationships, and our peace, will steadily improve in this life, that there will be rams in the thicket for us as we wait, importune, and receive the wonderful gift of hope.

1.   A. Theodore Tuttle, *Conference Report*, October 1967, 14–15.

2.   John Taylor, *Journal of Discourses* (London: Latter-day Saints' Book Depot, 1854–86), 17 March 1872, 14:360.

3.   Ibid., 14:359.

4. Joseph Fielding McConkie, *Gospel Symbolism* (Salt Lake City: Bookcraft, 1999), 153.

5. John Taylor, *Journal of Discourses* (London: Latter-day Saints' Book Depot, 1854–86), 17 March 1872, 14:361.

6. B. H. Roberts, *The Life of John Taylor*, (Salt Lake City: Deseret Book, 2002), 12–13, 72–73.

7. Susan Easton Black, Unpublished class notes on The Life of John Taylor: Religion C 342, BYU Fall 1999.

Chapter 5
Catching the
Ram of Hope

THOUGH FEW SACRAMENT MEETING PROGRAMS contain talks about hope, our General Authorities often teach about the subject of hope at general conference. In 1999, Elder Russell M. Nelson of the Quorum of the Twelve comforted the Saints with the following statements:

> To each person ... I bring a message of hope. Regardless of how desperate things may seem, remember—we can always have hope ... I repeat—there is always hope. . . . Hope is part of our religion and is mentioned in one of the *Articles of Faith*: . . . "We *hope* all things". . . A correlation exists between hope and gratitude . . . Hope emanates from the Lord and it transcends the bounds of this mortal sphere . . . "hope springs eternal". . . Hope springs from him who is eternal . . . Hope centers in his Atonement . . . The opposite of hope is despair . . . If there is no hope in Christ, there is no recognition of a divine plan for the redemption of mankind. . . . When we know who we are and what God expects of us, we are filled with hope and made aware of our significant role in his great plan of happiness. . . . But if our hopes were narrowly confined to moments in mortality we should surely be disappointed.[1]

I would also suggest that if our hopes are only for the next life then we will be disappointed. We must also have hope in and for this life.

Moroni tells us, "Wherefore I would speak unto you that are of the Church." Notice that in this instance, Moroni is only speaking to those who are Church members. He also adds another qualification for his readers that those he will make promises to those are also "peaceable followers of Christ." To those who have met these two qualifications he promises, "And that have obtained a sufficient hope by which ye can enter into the rest of the Lord, from this time henceforth until ye shall rest with him in heaven" (Moroni 7:3).

Moroni promises we can enter into sufficient hope now from this time henceforth, in mortality, not just in the eternities. We must have hope in promised blessings and in good things to come. Elder Richard G. Scott of the Quorum of the Twelve Apostles is one who had such a hope in good things to come in this life. I love to tell Elder Scott's story in my classes at Brigham Young University. Some students who attend my classes look around and think that all their classmates must have come from a "perfect Latter-day Saint family." With that false assumption, they give up hope of becoming anything but ordinary, or even substandard, Church members. They assume in order to be Church-leadership material, they must have grown up in families where everything was in place spiritually. So when I instruct my "Teachings of the Living Prophets" classes about the background of Elder Richard G. Scott, some students are pleasantly surprised to learn how the gift of hope brought him from a less-than-perfect background to be an Apostle of the Lord.

Richard G. Scott grew up in home with caring parents; however, his father was not a Latter-day Saint and his mother was considered inactive. Elder Scott grew up not going to Church often, disliking meetings when he did, and felt "he was on the outside of things socially." What made the difference in his life was a girl who lived by the Young Women values long before they were recited each Sunday. When Richard Scott met Jeanene Watkins, he discovered she was all he had ever dreamed of finding in a wife and fell in love. He could tell she had deep feelings for him also, but she had priorities in place. She hoped for a certain future. [2]

One night when Richard and Jeanene were talking about the future, she carefully wove into the conversation an important fact—she would only marry a man who had served a worthy mission and who could take her to the temple. That was Jeanene's hope and expectation.

Elder Scott did not remember anything else she said that night. He had not thought much about a mission and did not understand much about temple marriage. Jeanene had been promised those blessings and she held on to that hope and would not let it go, although she had fallen in love with someone who seemed unconcerned about these qualifications.

Richard Scott went home from that date and could not think of anything else except Jeanene's statement about marrying a returned missionary in the temple. He was awake all night, he was not productive at the university the next day, and he soon found himself at the bishop's office, after praying about the importance of a mission. Jeanene's hope had softened Richard Scott's heart, and he came to realize that she would find someone else if he did not make the right choices. [3]

Jeanene courageously standing up for her dream—her hope of a temple marriage to a returned missionary, regardless of her present circumstances—made all the difference in their future lives together. Elder Scott later said, "I will never be able to thank her adequately for trusting in the Lord and not compromising her righteous dreams." [4] Soon Elder Scott left for Uruguay on a mission. His future wife, Jeanene Watkins, graduated the following June and left the day after for a mission of her own to the Northwestern states. My favorite part of the story: Richard G. Scott did not waste any time. Two weeks after he returned from his mission, he and Jeanene Watkins were married on July 16, 1953 in the Manti Temple. Jeanene's hope became reality.

For the Scotts, hope was more than wishful thinking or having a positive mental attitude. Hope was an absolute expectation that those things they had been promised by the Lord were absolute. As President James E. Faust, counselor in the First Presidency, tells us, we have a choice: We "either live in hope or [we] live in despair." [5] Despair and doubt are the antithesis of hope, and without hope we will find it difficult to endure to the end, let alone endure well.

Where does hope come from? President Faust suggests there are several "sources of hope beyond our own ability, learning, strength, and capacity." Those sources include the Holy Ghost, personal prayers, the scriptures, and priesthood blessings. They bring "trust in God's promises, [and] faith that if we act now, the desired blessings will be fulfilled in the future." [6]

Elder Jeffrey R. Holland counsels that there are times when we need to know that "things will improve," that we can look forward to something hopeful, and that we have a promise of "good things to come" (Hebrews 9:11). We must hold on, keep trying for "a future of 'better promises'" (Hebrews 8:6). Elder Holland comforts, "Some blessings come soon, some come late, and some don't come until heaven; but for those who embrace the gospel of Jesus Christ, *they come*." [7] In Proverbs we are told: "Hope deferred maketh the heart sick: but when the desire cometh, it is a tree of life" (Proverbs 13:12). The Lord does not want us to figuratively sit on our suitcases just waiting for Eternal Life. He wants us to have expectations of good things to come in mortality.

I have heard a saying all my life that contradicts this idea of expectations. It is a saying cross-stitched in samplers and adorns countless refrigerator magnets. The saying is "Bloom where you are planted." I think that many times this saying represents a false concept, suggesting that we are to be as helpless as plants. We must realize that more often than not, we are the gardeners of our lives. Although I do not have a green thumb, I know enough that if a plant is not growing or thriving, a good gardener can and will do something about it. Instead of simply "blooming where you are planted," sometimes what is really needed is repotting or transplanting. In the lives of Latter-day Saints, the main fertilizer for repotting is hope. One day, an aquaintance of mine was gardening and found some flowers refusing to bloom where they were planted in her yard. She thought there was not enough sun where they were struggling, so she dug them up and moved them, and the flowers soon flourished in the new spot. Likewise, if we are struggling to bloom where we are, we can always repot, move, and change. None of us need feel stuck in life. If needed, we can move to grow better elsewhere. The ultimate transplant was Jesus of Nazareth. The New Testament tells us that it was a common thought that nothing good could come out of Nazareth (John 1:46), yet it was He that arose on that third day. One of the messages of the gospel of Jesus Christ is that we can change, improve, and have hope for good things to come.

Another story that I feel lacks hope comes from *Dear Abby*. The gist of the story goes like this: Pretend you have always wanted to go to Italy. You love Italian food and the great works of Michelangelo. You cannot wait to see the David, the ceiling of the Sistine Chapel, and eat

Italian gelato in a gondola. So you save and plan to fulfill your dream of going to Italy, but when you get on the plane and are flying over the ocean, it is announced that your plane is going to Holland. You did not want to go to Holland. You wanted to go to Italy. This trip is not what you planned at all. But when you step off the plane, you find that Holland has wonderful things such as windmills and tulips, and you are pleasantly surprised and satisfied. [8]

My friend Elizabeth Clark said, "If I paid to go to Italy, and they dropped me in Holland, you can bet I would go see the airline and get to Italy as I was promised." Elizabeth changed this "Dear Abby" story for me, and when she did, it filled me with a brilliant hope. Hope proclaims that we do not have to settle. Elizabeth Clark knows about this concept. At one time in her life, after literally being hit by a garbage truck, she was told by doctors that she would never sit again. Even after such a prognosis, Elizabeth Clark persevered, cultivated hope, and had expectations of good things to come, and I have seen her sit through all three hours of her Church meetings. The Lord has and will keep his promises, and I have discovered that what I receive from the Lord is even amazingly better than for what I hoped.

One reason we hope for certain blessings, situations, and outcomes is because the Holy Ghost influences us through our preferences. There is divine design in the fact that we prefer one thing or one person over another and that we have certain desires. If we lose sight of our preferences, hopes, dreams, and promises, we will experience despair. In my life it has been those hopes, dreams, and promises that have helped me to have trust in a bright future. As Sheri L. Dew, former counselor in the General Relief Society Presidency, instructed students at Brigham Young University, "You were born to lead. You were born to build Zion. You were born for glory. Everything you do in life should be measured against this grand standard." [9] Isaiah wrote that we are to be a standard to the people of the world (Isaiah 49:22). Our charge is to dispel the darkness of this world with hope.

The standard for Latter-day Saints is one of glory. After all, our Heavenly Father's plan is called "the plan of happiness," not the plan of settling. We cannot be satisfied with our circumstances if they are not what the Spirit has directed us to become.

The great American psychologist William James declared, "The greatest discovery of my generation is that human beings can alter their lives by altering the attitudes of mind." [10] This statement had a profound affect on future prophet David O. McKay. He recalls being "a little shaken" when he took psychology as a college student, but William James, "the psychologist, however, recognized that the field of spirituality was beyond him. His honest attitude helped me during the period of doubt and hasty conclusions characteristic of youth." From the starting point of James' statement President McKay declared that,

> The most real thing to me in all my existence, is my thought. And what you are thinking, whatever it may be, is the most real to you in this world at this moment. You can analyze your brain and catch the explosion in the brain which seems to produce the thought, but the thought is yours, as literally as the coat you are wearing or any physical part of your being. . . . I know that thought, or feeling of awareness may be sensed independent of these five senses. The spirit in man has its position, and controls this physical body just as the driver of an auto may control that machine. Just so, may man be controlled. The spirit may become cognizant of an event prior to its happening, or which is beyond the limit of these five senses. . . . And so, it is finding and trailing this spiritual contact with the infinite. God is pulling us back into His presence. If you have ever felt the touch of inspiration, you will know that what I say is true. [11]

Our thoughts can control our future lives. Elder Royden Derrick of the First Quorum of the Seventy confirms, "God does not select the type of life we live. We make that selection by what we think. If you want to play the part, just act the part." [12]

As Elder Derrick explained above, we decide the type of life we will live. In a large way, we control our own circumstances and destiny. This was true of the early Saints of this dispensation. In June 1834, the Saints in Missouri were told that in consequence of their transgression they would have to wait a little season for the redemption of Zion (D&C 105:9). Most have assumed that "a little season" is a lot different in the Lord's timing than ours. We are still waiting and have been for over 160 years to fully redeem Missouri, or the central stake of Zion. However, this season did not have to be so long. In a letter Joseph Smith wrote, the Lord specifically told the Saints in Missouri that if they were faithful, prayerful, and humble, and would not boast of their strength they could be back in Missouri by September 11, 1839. [13] Had those Saints in Missouri followed the Lord's counsel, if they would have held to their hopes, Latter-day Saints would be thriving in the Center Stake of Zion in Missouri today. Fortunately, the Lord had a contingency plan and we will yet redeem Zion. What former Dean of Religious Education Robert Millet stated was true of the Missouri Saints in 1839, "Most of the time we do not see things as they really are; we see things as we really are." [14] With hope we can repot, transplant, arise and shine as Zion, and see things as they really are instead of how things appear at any particular moment in time.

My father was one whose attitude changed his future. During the 1920s, his parents were divorced in a day when most marriages did not end in divorce. My grandfather valued athletic ability, and it soon became apparent that my uncle had athletic abilities and my dad did not. As these two brothers grew up, my father felt my uncle was favored. My father remembered that my grandfather would pick my uncle up, take him to ball games, and leave my father as a young boy standing at the window watching. My father did not try to bloom in that athletic garden; instead, he repotted by transplanting himself where his preference led. When such disappointments would come, he would deal with it by pounding on the piano. According to my dad, by the time these two boys were teenagers, it was not my athletic uncle who was the life of the party. Where they grew up in Magrath, Alberta, Canada, there was not much to do, so at parties someone would say to my father, "Winston, do you know such and such a song?" He would reply, "No, but if you hum it I can play it." As a musician, my father became a very popular personality at socials.

Along these same lines, one of my favorite stories from my father's life was when he was being inducted into the army. He found himself in a large hall with several other men in their "skivvies" waiting for a physical, when he spotted a piano in the corner of the hall, went over to it, and started to play. He had to wait a long time for his physical because the inductees were called alphabetically, and his last name started with a W. As he waited, he played the piano and entertained those future troops. During his physical the doctor turned to my father and asked, "Did you know you are deaf in your right ear?"

My father replied, "I thought maybe I was," and he was "4Fd" out of the military during World War II. It was highly unlikely that my father would bloom in a musical garden, and yet that was the way my dad arose and shone forth, first on the piano, then as a truly great conductor. He had hopes, and through the Lord's help, succeeded in achieving his dreams.

Another story laden with hope is recorded in Matthew 15:21. There was a certain woman whose young daughter had an unclean spirit. In our modern language we would say her daughter had a mental or emotional illness. She might have been dealing with depression, been bipolar, or even been schizophrenic. This mother had heard of Christ's healings and sought the Savior. We see this woman as a rather intuitive person to even find Him, as she inappropriately showed up right at mealtime. Seeking solitude Jesus had escaped the crowds, and she interrupted his few minutes of rest asking for help in behalf of her daughter.

The woman was a citizen of a Greek nation, a Syrophoenician by birth. In short, she was the wrong gender, the wrong citizenship, and the wrong ethnic background. She was not blooming where she was planted; she was doing a major transplant as she accepted Jesus as her promised Messiah. She cried, "Have mercy on me, O Lord, thou Son of David; my daughter is grievously vexed with a devil" (Matthew 15:22). But Jesus answered her not a word. He does not say a thing. She seems to not be offended by his silence, or if she is, she simply chooses not to let it bother her. Chagrined at her impulsiveness, Christ's disciples suggest sending her away. The Savior does not succumb to their request. It is important to remember that He does not ask her to leave. He does not send us away either, even when you and I, like this woman, ask for things that are inappropriate or outside of the garden where we are planted. He responded to her patience, "I am not sent but unto the lost sheep of the house of Israel" (Matthew 15:24). She keeps importuning, and then Matthew used the word worshipping. When answers do not come, do we importune, do we keep worshipping, do we keep hoping? "Lord, help me," she cried (Matthew 15:25). He replied, "It is not meet to take the children's bread, and cast it to dogs" (Matthew 15:26). Here some might accuse the Lord of being rude. In this instance, one of my colleagues even called him mean. I would disagree with that judgment because He is the only one to have lived on this earth who truly does not have a mean bone in his body. He is not calling this woman names. Instead, he is trying to help her understand her position, where she is supposed to bloom. What is her reaction? She replied, "Truth, Lord; yet the dogs eat of the crumbs which fall from their masters' table" (Matthew 15:27). In other words, she is saying, "This is what I want, but if you have much less in mind for right now I'll wait."

The Lord displays no condescension; instead, I believe He is giving a test of faith and patience to this mother. It was a test she passed with flying colors. Then Jesus said, "O woman, great is thy faith: be it unto thee even as thou wilt. And her daughter was made whole from that very hour" (Matthew 15:28). Because she was content to accept the Lord's will, he eventually gave her the desires of her heart. Although she was not entitled as a non-member of the house of Israel to a miracle at that time, through her hope she was given a blessing. We are not entitled to the desires of our hearts, but the Lord often blesses us with what we may not deserve by ourselves but qualify for through His gracious Atonement. As Sheri L. Dew tells us about such tests like this New Testament woman experienced, "Challenges that tax our faith are usually opportunities to stretch and strengthen our faith by finding out if we really believe the Lord will help us."[15]

Our generation does not worship God by the title of Jehovah as found in the Old Testament. There will be no Moses to take us on an exodus. There will be no Joshua to kill all that tempts us. There is no wilderness left; instead we are planted right in the middle of modern Sodom. We instead must worship a "high priest of good things to come" (Hebrews 9:11). I cannot give up on desires, dreams, or hopes, because when I do, when I am told to just be happy where I am at, I do not arise or shine. We will arise by holding dear to those dreams, desires, and wants. Elder Holland has comforted:

> Through his mediation and atonement, Christ became "an high priest of good things to come." Every one of us has times when we need to know things will get better. . . . For emotional health and spiritual stamina, everyone needs to be able to look forward to some respite, to something pleasant and renewing and hopeful, whether that blessing be near at hand or still some distance ahead. It is enough just to know we can get

there, that however measured or far away, there is
the promise of "good things to come.". . . There *is*
help. There *is* happiness . . . Hold on. Keep trying.
God loves you. Things will improve. Christ comes
to you . . . with a future of "better promises." He is
your "high priest of good things to come.". . . Christ
knows better than all others that the trials of life can
be very deep and we are not shallow people if we
struggle with them.[16]

President Gordon B. Hinckley has promised Latter-day Saints,
"You have the potential to become anything to which you set your
mind to." Your mind, body, and spirit can work together to lead you to
achievement and happiness if you make the necessary effort and sacrifice
using your faith.[17] As Church Educator, S. Michael Wilcox reminds us,
"Hope manifests itself in various ways in different people. . . . Hope is
a guide, a protection, a source of nourishment, and a stabilizing force
for our lives. . . . Hope must have substance to it."[18] Hope removes a
sense of hurry; it tells us there is always sufficient time. Hope truly
believes that all things will be for our good (D&C 111:11). I use that
very phrase in my prayers sometimes to increase my hope when I am
going through something difficult. I pray, "Heavenly Father, this does
not seem quite right, but please let it turn for my good." In like fashion, Elder Orson F. Whitney of the Quorum of the Twelve Apostles
promised:

No pain that we suffer, no trial that we experience is
wasted. It ministers to our education, to the development of such qualities as patience, faith, fortitude, and
humility. All that we suffer and all that we endure,
especially when we endure it patiently, builds up our
character, purifies our hearts, expands our souls, and
makes us more tender and charitable, more worthy
to be called the children of God . . . and it is through
sorrow and suffering, toil and tribulation, that we gain
the education that we come here to acquire and which
will make us more like our Father.[19]

Hope overcomes even the greatest of obstacles and knows that
sometimes the Lord does his best work when it seems almost impossible. As Elder Russell M. Nelson shared in this hopeful insight:

Have you ever wondered why the Master waited so long to inaugurate the promised "restitution of all things" (Acts 3:21)? Any competitor knows the disadvantage of allowing an opponent to get too far ahead. Wouldn't the work of the restoration of the Church have been easier if begun earlier?

Suppose for a moment you are a member of a team. The coach beckons you from the bench and says: "You are to enter this contest. I not only want you to win; you shall win. But the going will be tough. The score at this moment is 1,143,000,000 to six, and you are to play on the team with the six points!"

That large number was the approximate population of the earth in the year 1830 when the restored church of Jesus Christ was officially organized with six members. [20]

Even against such impossible odds, hope can be constant. Elder John H. Groberg describes hope in this way, "There is always hope. No matter how dismal things appear, no matter how problem-prone we seem to be, no matter what reversals and setbacks we suffer, there is always hope. Hope is the thing that keeps us going." [21] As we sing in the hymn *We Thank Thee Oh God for a Prophet,* "When dark clouds of trouble hang o'er us / And threaten our peace to destroy, / There is hope smiling brightly before us / And we know that deliverance is nigh." Do we really believe the words of that hymn? Do we believe deliverance is nigh? The thirteenth article of faith declares: "We believe all things, we hope all things." Those who have hope know that God is fair, and they trust him. They know that in the end and the middle, they will find many happy surprises. [22]

Ultimate hope is in the Atonement of Jesus Christ. [23] Having that ultimate hope permits us to "rejoice in the many blessings we now have without brooding over those that are temporarily withheld from us." It "permits us to deal more evenly with the unevenness of life's experiences." [24] However, even with a solid testimony of the atonement, as Elder Maxwell instructs, some of us struggle with having hope for the future.

We may actually acknowledge God's past blessings but still fear that He will not deliver us in a present situation. Or we may trust that God will finally deliver us but fear He will do so only after a severe trial which we desperately do not want! . . . . Inwardly and anxiously we may worry, too, that an omniscient and loving God sees more stretch in us than we feel we have. Hence when God is actually lifting us up, we may feel He is letting us down. . . . having sufficient faith to lead a vibrant, daily life here in mortality.

We can learn the important difference between passing, local cloud cover, and general darkness. We can "hold out," if we but hold on by maintaining our perspective. But while we are in the midst of "all these things," the very experiences which can be for our long-term good, the anguish is real. We may feel, for instance, that some trials are simply more than we can bear. Yet, if we have faith in God's character as an all-knowing and all-loving Father, we understand that in His plan He will not give us more than we can bear. (See 1 Corinthians 10:13; D&C 50:40.)

In 480 B.C. a small Greek force under the Spartan king Leonidas courageously held a mountain pass for three days at a place called Thermopylae against overwhelming numbers of the enemy. When someone commented that the Persian army was so huge that their arrows blocked out the sun, one of the defenders replied: "So much the better. We shall fight in the shade!" [25]

Such wonderful hope that delivered the Spartans can also deliver us from the confines of our personal battles, even battling despair from becoming our companion in mortality. President Lorenzo Snow saw that battling despair sooner or later is part of the mortal experience. He penned these lines:

All who journey soon or late
Must come within the garden gate,
And kneel alone in darkness there,
And battle hard, yet not despair. [26]

Keeping hope alive is sometimes a hard battle, but in the struggle, we will be blessed to not despair. Ether 12:4 reads, "Hope cometh of faith, maketh an anchor to the souls of men, which would make them sure and steadfast, always abounding in good works."

Hope Is Not

To understand the concept of hope, it is valuable to understand what it is not. Elder Neal A. Maxwell gives us a list of antonyms for hope as follows:

> Real hope is much more than wishful musing. If stiffens, not slackens, the spiritual spine. Hope is serene, not giddy, eager without being naïve, and pleasantly steady without being smug. Hope is realistic anticipation which takes the form of a determination—not only to survive adversity, but, moreover, to "endure . . . well" to the end . . . Indeed when we are unduly impatient with an omniscient God's timing, we really are suggesting that we know what is best. Strange, isn't it—that we who wear wrist-watches seek to counsel Him who oversees cosmic clocks and calendars. [27]

Our wanting immediate deliverance from suffering suggests we have greater confidence in our own timetable than in His, and we may suffer much longer than is necessary simply because we do not know that hope can free us from pain. [28]

In addition, hope is not advanced when we compare ourselves with others. The hopeful do not focus on failures and weaknesses; instead, they focus on victories and the good deeds of their lives. Those without hope exhibit downheartedness, they are disturbed. I would suggest that you can measure the level of hope you have in the Savior by the depth and frequency of depression and discouragement you sink to.

In our modern society, it is sometimes difficult to retain hope. Stress is one of the common elements of modern life. There is such a thing as positive stress which motivates us to eat when hungry or sleep when tired. But continual, unrelieved frustration, hostility or resentment called distress is an accurate predictor of heart attacks and other health and behavioral problems. Prolonged distress suppresses our bodies' immune systems that provide natural defenses against infections and other diseases. "Distress and peace are mutually exclusive—they cannot coexist."[29] Neither can distress and hope. Elder Neal A. Maxwell teaches that,

> Doubt and despair go together, whereas faith and hope are constant companions. . . . When we have appropriate hope of receiving eternal life (Alma 13:29), and we retain that hope through faith (Alma 25:16), then we will—even though we love life, family, and friends—have "no terror of death" "because of [our] hope and views of Christ and the resurrection." (Alma 27:28) Indeed, true hope springs directly from our "views of Christ.". . . However, our hope, unless it is strong, can be at the mercy of our moods and can be badgered and bullied by events and by the contempt of the world, which we will experience in rather large doses in the irreligious last part of the last dispensation.

Without hope we become "unduly impatient" with the Lord.

> The true believer can read the depressing signs of the times without being depressed, because he has a particularized and "perfect brightness of hope," and he knows that Christ will lift him up . . . Besides, the true believer knows that in the awful winding-up scenes, human deterioration will be finally and decisively met by Divine intervention.[30]

"We are at our most self-centered state when we are depressed."[31] Nothing can sap our natural strength and health as much as prolonged depression because it is based on the lie of hopelessness. When depressed, we focus on our powerlessness and deny the hope of Christ's deliverance and strength. However, as Elder John H. Groberg suggests, hope is never completely gone. We are never hopeless:

> One of Satan's ultimate weapons (if not the ultimate) is to remove hope from your life. He tries to convince you that you can't do it, that there is no hope. Thus,

by removing hope, he removes Christ from your life, for Christ is hope. Satan can never quite accomplish that fully—at least not here—because it is a lie. There is hope built within all of us. There is always hope.

On the other hand, the thing Satan cannot fight is one who is full of hope—for he is then full of the Spirit of Christ—and when that hope is perfected or full, Satan has lost completely. [32]

When we are faced with darkness, disease, death, betrayal, or false accusations, Satan whispers there must be something wrong with us. He whispers that you and I are not okay, or bad things would not be happening to us. [33] Facing these lies, many get caught up in unwise or extreme therapies. In addition, "modern music, movies, and books reflect a sense of growing despair and disbelief." [34] However, within the framework of the gospel of Jesus Christ, we can do things to counteract the growing despair around us and develop hope.

Developing Hope by Giving Encouragement to Others

Imagine what it would have been like for Joseph Smith if, in addition to everything else he suffered, he had been constantly ridiculed and persecuted by his immediate family members. Joseph Smith's siblings were a constant source of hope, and as they gave encouragement to their brother, in turn the Lord instilled hope in them. Giving hope to each other was a Smith family trait handed down through generations.

In 1799, when each of his four married children were about to present him with a new grandchild, Asael Smith, grandfather of the prophet Joseph Smith, wrote "a few words of advice" to his family:

> My last request and charge is that you will live together in an undivided bond of love. You are many of you, and if you join together as one man, you need not want anything. What counsel, what comfort, what money, what friends may you not help yourselves unto, if you will all as one contribute your aids. Wherefore my

dear children, I pray, beseech, and adjure you by all the relations and dearness that hath ever been betwixt us and by the heart-rending pangs of a dying father, whose soul hath been ever bound in the bundle of life with yours, that you know one another. Visit as you may each other. Comfort, counsel, relieve, succor, help and admonish one another. And while your mother lives, meet her if possible once every year. When she is dead, pitch on some other place, if it may be, your elder brother's house; or if you cannot meet, send to and hear from each other yearly and oftener if you can. And when you have neither father nor mother left, be so many fathers and mothers to each other. [35]

Such giving of "comfort, counsel, relief, succor, and hope" was passed on to the next generation. Elder M. Russell Ballard tells us that Hyrum Smith consistently served as a source of hope to his brother.

Through it all, Hyrum stood firm. He knew the course his life would take, and he consciously chose to follow it. To Joseph, Hyrum became companion, protector, provider, confidant, and eventually joined him as a martyr. Unjust persecution engulfed them throughout their lives. Although he was older, Hyrum recognized his brother's divine mantle. While he gave Joseph strong counsel on occasion, Hyrum always deferred to his younger brother.

Speaking to his brother, Joseph once said, "Brother Hyrum, what a faithful heart you have got! Oh may the Eternal Jehovah crown eternal blessings upon your head, as a reward for the care you have had for my soul! O how many are the sorrows we have shared together." [36]

Joseph was able to rely on his family for support, encouragement, strength, and hope. When we care for another's soul as Hyrum cared for his younger brother, hope in our own lives grows. As Elder Maxwell taught, "We create each other's opportunities for giving—like it or not! Hope filled souls do not crave affliction or seeming tragedy, but they will use all such circumstances for their eternal good." [37]

Acting as if Blessings Have Already Been Given Develops Hope

There is a scriptural mandate to act as if blessings have already happened. This is clear in many places, especially through Book of Mormon prophets who spoke of things to come as if they had already happened. "And now if Christ had not come into the world, speaking of things to come as though they had already come, there could have been no redemption" (Mosiah 16:6).

Christ gives the same example. Before he went to Gethsemane he told his disciples to "be of good cheer; I have overcome the world" (John 16:33). Yet chronologically when He made this statement, His trials of Gethsemane and the cross were just about to happen. He knew he would complete His work. Prophets also see their reality as God sees it—life for them is a "constant now." Speaking of such a prophetic stance, playwright Thornton Wilder penned these words, "It is only in appearance that time is a river. It is rather a vast landscape and it is the eye of the beholder that moves."[38] Blurring the timeline in the Lord's promises produces hope.

Patricia Holland of the Young Women general presidency shows us this same concept in the following:

> As I tenderly acknowledge the very real pain that many single women, or married women who have not borne children, feel . . . could we consider this one possibility about our eternal female identity . . . ? Eve was given the identity of "the mother of all living" years, decades, perhaps centuries before she ever bore a child. It would appear that her motherhood preceded her maternity, just as surely as the perfection of the Garden preceded the struggles of mortality.[39]

Recently I was told that when I am discouraged, I should ask for the gift of prophecy. "Hope does the seeing, albeit through glass darkly, but it is patience that sees us through."[40] We are to covet the gift of prophecy. Such a practice produces hope.

Keeping the Commandments
Produces Hope

Keeping the commandments increases hope whereas disobedience destroys it. Elder Neal A. Maxwell exhorts:

> Another of the consequences of gross sexual immorality with its desensitization is that it begins to rob man of hope. As an individual is emptied of hope, despair quickly enters in for as one prophet said, "Despair cometh because of iniquity" (Moroni 10:22). Thus wickedness and despair are terrifying and self-reinforcing. [41]

On the other hand, obedience to the commandments brings hope that our desires will be blessed. One great example of faithful Latter-day Saints being blessed with their hopes because of faithful obedience took place in the last decades of the twentieth century. During the communist regime in East Germany, Latter-day Saints were denied many blessings. On April 27, 1975, President Thomas S. Monson promised the Latter-day Saints in East Germany the "entire program of the Church" including temple blessings when such a thing seemed impossible. President Monson based his prayerful request as being merited by the East German Saints and their obedience. Notice how President Monson made his request for these blessings to come within the framework of the Saints' faithfulness in keeping the commandments in his dedication of East Germany.

> Thou knowest the faith of the people of this land— the many tens of thousands who have embraced Thy gospel and have served to build up Thy church wherever they have been. Thou knowest the sermons which they have preached in song, for they sing with their hearts and echo the feelings of their souls.
>
> Thou knowest, Heavenly Father, the sufferings of this people, and Thou hast been near to them in times of trouble and in times of joy.

We express our gratitude unto Thee for the privilege we have of holding meetings here, for bringing to the membership of the Dresden Mission the entire program of the Church. These blessings were scarcely imaginable a few years ago. We confess before Thee that it has been through Thy intervention that this blessing has been brought to pass. We acknowledge thy hand in every aspect of our lives and pledge our lives to Thy service. . . .

Grant that the children of the membership of the Church in the Dresden Mission may be loyal to Thy cause, and the grandchildren, even unto the last generation before the second coming of Thy Beloved Son. Grant, Heavenly Father, that the membership here may receive their patriarchal blessings and live in such a way as to bring the promises to fulfillment.

Heavenly Father, wilt Thou open up the way that the faithful may be accorded the privilege of going to Thy holy temple, there to receive their holy endowments and to be sealed as families for time and all eternity. . . .

Grant that the way may be cleared for the program of the Church in its fullness to come to this people, for they, through their faith, have merited such blessings. [42]

Like these East German Saints, our obedience to God's commandments will also merit us the blessing of hope.

Participating in Ordinances Brings Hope

Elder Neal A. Maxwell tells us the "ordinances show our visible outward obedience to the Lord and his plan of salvation . . . Ordinances are intended to cast our minds forward to specific promises and to our developmental possibilities." [43] Participating in ordinances, especially in the house of the Lord, increases our hope for promised blessings. When we participate in ordinances it is important to "look beyond the limited behaviors themselves to focus on the limitless meanings and significance the behaviors represent. Keeping the broader perspective, searching for eternal implications in the otherwise mortal motions is paramount."[44] Part of that broader perspective will also include an enlarged degree of hope.

Coming unto Jesus Christ Produces Hope

One trip to a temple had a memorable impact on my life. On the last leg of a business trip, I found myself alone in Preston, England, one summer weekend. I had attended the temple and was staying in the accommodations next to the temple over a Sunday, waiting for an early flight on Monday morning. Much to my surprise, no one else was staying in the lodgings, and on that Sunday after Church meetings, I was left to spend the rest of the day alone. Not knowing anyone in Preston, I felt isolated and depressed over some situations I would go home to. That Sunday afternoon I took a long walk and finally ended up back at the LDS Church building adjacent to the temple. There was a priesthood leader in an office conducting interviews, but no one else was in the building. I ventured into the Relief Society room and began to play hymns on the piano. As I was turning pages, I found a hymn I never remembered hearing before and the words were very poignant to my situation.

Come unto Him

> I wander through the still of night,
> When solitude is ev'rywhere—
> Alone, beneath the starry light,
> And yet I know that God is there.
> I kneel upon the grass and pray;
> An answer comes without a voice.
> It takes my burden all away
> And makes my aching heart rejoice.

When I am filled with strong desire
And ask a boon of him, I see
No miracle of living fire,
But what I ask flows into me.
And when the tempest rages high
I feel no arm around me thrust,
But ev'ry storm goes rolling by
When I repose in him my trust.

It matters not what may befall,
What threat'ning hand hangs over me;
He is my rampart through it all,
My refuge from mine enemy.
Come unto him all ye depressed,
Ye erring souls whose eyes are dim,
Ye weary ones who long for rest.
Come unto him! Come unto him![45]

As I read those last words "Come unto Him all ye depressed . . . Ye weary ones who long for rest. Come unto Him," I was filled with a sweet feeling of succor and solace, realizing that we are never really alone. Those who come unto Him will feel His rest, repose, and rejoice in the hope that He gives us.

1. Russell M. Nelson, "A More Excellent Hope," *Ensign* (February 1997), 60–63.

2. Lynne Hollstein, "Harmony of Truth Inspires Him to do Will of Lord" *Deseret News*, 30 April 1977, 7.

3. *Church News*, 30 April 1977, 7.

4. Richard G. Scott, "Do What Is Right," *Ensign* (June 1997), 52.

5. James E. Faust, "Hope, an Anchor of the Soul," *Ensign* (November 1999), 59.

6. Ibid., 59–60. See Romans 4:18–21.

7. Jeffrey R. Holland, "An High Priest of Good Things to Come," *Ensign* (November 1999), 36 and 38.

8. Emily Pearl Kingsley, "Welcome to Holland," http://www.journeyofhearts.org/jofh/kirstimd/holland.htm [accessed 23 June 2005]. (Dear Abby reprints it as part of the National Down Syndrome Awareness Month)

9. Sheri Dew, "Born to Glory," *BYU Magazine* (Spring 2004), 38.

10. Richard L. Evans, *Richard Evans' Quote Book* (Salt Lake City: Publishers Press, 1971), 161.

11. Deseret News *Church News*, August 1936, 1.

12. Royden G. Derrick, "Valiance in the Drama of Life," *Ensign* (May 1983), 24.

13. B. H. Roberts, ed., *History of the Church of Jesus Christ of Latter-day Saints*, 2d ed., rev. (Salt Lake City: Deseret Book, 1978), 2:144–45.

14. Robert L. Millet, *Alive in Christ: The Miracle of Spiritual Birth* (Salt Lake City: Deseret Book, 1997), 28.

15. Sheri Dew, "Born to Glory," *BYU Magazine* (Spring 2004), 36.

16. Jeffrey R. Holland, "An High Priest of Good Things to Come," *Ensign*, November 1999, 36–37.

17. Gordon B. Hinckley, "Stay on the High Road," *Ensign*, May 2004, 113.

18. S. Michael Wilcox, *Hope an Anchor to the Soul* (Salt Lake City: Deseret Book, 1999), 1–2, and 5.

19. Orson F. Whitney as quoted by Spencer W. Kimball, *Faith Precedes the Miracle* (Salt Lake City: Deseret Book, 1972), 98.

20. Russell M. Nelson, "With God Nothing Shall Be Impossible," *Ensign*, May 1988, 33–34. See also James Avery Joyce, ed., *World Population Basic Documents*, 4 vols., (Dobbs Ferry: Oceana Publications, 1976), 4:2214.

21. John H. Groberg, "There is Always Hope," *Hope* (Salt Lake City: Deseret Book, 1994), 46.

22. Garth L. Allred, *Unlocking the Powers of Faith* (American Fork: Covenant Communications, 1993), 65.

23. Neal A. Maxwell, "Hope through the Atonement of Jesus Christ," *Ensign*, November 1998, 61.

24. Neal A. Maxwell, "The Christ-Centered Life," *Ensign*, August 1981, 16 and Neal A. Maxwell, "Hope through the Atonement of Jesus Christ," *Ensign*, November 1998, 61.

25. Neal A. Maxwell, *Lord, Increase Our Faith* (Salt Lake City: Bookcraft, 1994), 3, 7, 43–44, and 51.

26. John Taylor, *Journal of Discourses* (London: Latter-day Saints' Book Depot, 1854–86), 10 January 1886, 26:367.

27. Neal A. Maxwell, "Hope through the Atonement of Jesus Christ," *Ensign*, November 1998, 62–63.

28. Garth L. Allred, *Unlocking the Powers of Faith* (American Fork: Covenant Communications, 1993), 64.

29. Ibid., 59.

30. Neal A. Maxwell, *Notwithstanding My Weakness* (Salt Lake City: Deseret Book, 1981), 41, 44, 45, and 124.

31. Garth L. Allred, *Unlocking the Powers of Faith* (American Fork: Covenant Communications, 1993), 105.

32. John H. Groberg, "There Is Always Hope," *Hope* (Salt Lake City: Deseret Book, 1994), 52.

33. Garth L. Allred, *Unlocking the Powers of Faith* (American Fork: Covenant Communications, 1993), 105.

34. Neal A. Maxwell, *Lord, Increase Our Faith* (Salt Lake City: Deseret Book, 1994), 59.

35. Richard Lloyd Anderson, *Joseph Smith's New England Heritage: Influences of Grandfathers Solomon Mack and Asael Smith* (Salt Lake City: Deseret Book, 1971), 163–64.

36. M. Russell Ballard, "Hyrum Smith: 'Firm As the Pillars of Heaven,' " *Ensign*, November 1995, 6–7.

37. Neal A. Maxwell, *Notwithstanding My Weakness* (Salt Lake City: Deseret Book, 1981), 55.

38. Thornton Wilder, *The Eighth Day* (New York: Harper & Row, 1967), 395.

39. Jeffrey R. Holland and Patricia T. Holland, *On Earth As It Is in Heaven* (Salt Lake City: Deseret Book, 1989), 94.

40. Neal A. Maxwell, *Notwithstanding My Weakness* (Salt Lake City: Deseret Book, 1981), 58.

41. Ibid., 97.

42. Thomas S. Monson, *Faith Rewarded: A Personal Account of Prophetic Promises to the East German Saints* (Salt Lake City: Deseret Book, 1996, 35–37.

43. Neal A. Maxwell, *Lord, Increase Our Faith* (Salt Lake City: Bookcraft, 1994), 74 and 76.

44. Richard L. Bednar and Scott R. Peterson, *Spirituality and Self-Esteem: Developing the Inner Self* (Salt Lake City: Deseret Book, 1990), 129.

45. Hymns, "Come unto Him," no. 114, Text: Theodore E. Curtis (1872–1957), Music: Hugh W. Dougall (1872–1963).

Chapter 6

Receiving the Greatest Gift

THE ATTRIBUTE OF CHARITY IS DIFFICULT TO GRASP. This spiritual gift is the pinnacle of all gifts and Moroni tells us "whoso is found possessed of it at the last day, it shall be well with him" (Moroni 7:47). There are few mortals who have consistently and constantly experienced the possession of charity. In fact, there is only one who has dwelled on the earth who got charity "right." Elder Jeffery R. Holland tells us of the rarity of charity:

> True charity, the absolutely, pure perfect love of Christ, has really been known only once in this world—in the form of Christ Himself the loving Son of the living God. . . . As in everything Christ, is the only one who got it all right, did it all perfectly, loved the way we are all to try to love. But even though we fall short, that divine standard is there for us. It is a goal toward which we are to keep reaching, keep striving—and certainly a goal to keep appreciating. [1]

The divine standard of charity was provided by the Lord during His earth life. In addition, there are also some mortals we can use as role models who possess a fair measure of charity and often love others as Christ would.

I learned a lot about charity from two people who loved me. Parental love can come close to Christ-like love. Marjorie Pay Hinckley, wife of the Prophet Gordon B. Hinckley, once said of parents, "No one will ever love you as much. Your husband will love you, your wife will love you, but let me disillusion you right now—it will not be the way your mother and father love you. Theirs is as close to an unselfish love as we know on this earth."[2] Because I was loved by two mortals without reservation, I can conceive of my Savior's and my Heavenly Father's love for me being unqualified. I refer to this love as unqualified rather than unconditional. As Elder Russell M. Nelson has taught, "While divine love [charity] can be called perfect, infinite, enduring, and universal, it cannot correctly be characterized as *unconditional*. The word does not appear in the scriptures. On the contrary, many verses affirm that the higher levels of love the Father and the Son feel for each of us—and certain divine blessings stemming from that love—are *conditional*."[3] Elder Nelson instead refers to God's love as unqualified. The experience below is just one of many which took place during my developmental years, where I experienced the charity of my parents that was sometimes both undeserved and unqualified.

While I was growing up, a couple involved in the dairy industry sponsored a high school senior girl in our ward every year to compete in the county dairy princess contest each year. The year I graduated from high school, they sponsored me. I was thrilled with the anticipation of becoming a Dairy Princess and even practiced my parade wave. However, as the pageant loomed near, I became concerned about being asked a question during the evening gown competition as I had seen in the Miss America pageant, and I discussed this concern with my father. Wisely, my dad counseled, "Let me teach you a quote and no matter what they ask, this quote can be a part of the answer and you will be very impressive being able to quote something off the top of your head." The quote he taught me by Ralph Waldo Emerson was oft repeated by Heber J. Grant: "That which we persist in doing becomes easier for us to do; not that the nature of the thing itself is changed, but that our power to do is increased." Taking my father's advice to heart, I memorized the quote and left for the pageant feeling confident that I could answer any question.

As the pageant progressed to the evening gown competition and the master of ceremonies began to ask questions, I knew I was in trouble. Much to my surprise, he was not asking the types of questions I had heard on the Miss America pageants. Instead, he was asking questions about the milk and dairy industry. When the Master of Ceremonies got to me he asked, "Tell us about the process of pasteurization and explain how it has advanced the dairy industry." I had been studying root words in my English class and recognized the word "pasture" in pasteurization, but other than that I drew a complete blank. Looking down at my father I remembered he had promised that I could use his quote no matter what I was asked. So I replied, "Well pasteurization has to do with the cows going out to the pasture. The more you pasture a cow the better they pasteurize not because pasteurization gets easier but as the cows persist pasturing, it becomes easier not because the nature of pasteurization has changed but because the cows ability to pasteurize has increased." Most of the audience began to laugh. Amidst the laughter, I looked down and saw my father. He had his hand over his eyes and was shaking his head in embarrassment. Being intelligent was very important to my father, and he expected his children to be, or at least appear, intelligent also. I had just proved that for my part, this was not the case. Needless to say, I didn't win the title of Dairy Princess.

After the pageant, my father went home in his car. I changed my clothes, and went out to get in my car when I saw a note from my dad on the front windshield which he had quickly written on the back of a deposit slip. It simply said, "Janie, I still love you. See you at home, dad." That was always the message from my parents, "I love you no matter what you do." Such was the unqualified, unreserved love of my earthly father.

My father knew that the greatest knowledge a patriarch gives to his children is the knowledge that they are loved. Included in that type of message, a child not only learns that his or her parents love them without reservation, but they can also transfer that knowledge to understand that a Heavenly Father also loves them in the same way. Symbolically, there is a note from our Father in Heaven always waiting for us which states, "I still love you; I'll see you at home." That feeling of being loved inculcates self-esteem. In her book *Confronting the Myth of Self-Esteem*, Ester Rasband's explains:

> When we are loved, we learn that to the person who loves us, *it doesn't matter whether we are lovable or not.* Our behavior may hurt and disappoint; consequences will have to be paid. Nevertheless, the source of love—our security base—is utterly dependable, notwithstanding our weakness. . . . We love not because someone is lovable but because we are able to love. [4]

We are cared for in the way described above by a loving Father in Heaven. We will always be loved by our Father in Heaven. In the premortal existence, we knew we were loved to this extent. We were absolutely secure in the complete covering of parental love. We knew we were a favorite of our Father in Heaven. As is sung in the musical "The Slipper and the Rose," we may also say,

> Once I was loved
> I knew I was loved
> I flew through my days
> In fanciful ways
> Secure and sure there'd always be
> endless love for me

But with the veil some of us feel that

> Gone is that love
> My fanciful dove
> Has tears in her eyes
> She no longer flies
> And yet my heart will not despair
> For it's there
> Just [an answered prayer] away

> Once I was loved
> But always come what may
> [Heavenly Father's] constant memory
> Ever will be loving me [5]

Ultimately, our Father in Heaven's love or charity for us is a gift. In our premortal existence, that gift was felt and completely immersed our spirits in a sense of well-being. We were safe and secure in our existence. Our eternal identities, that part of us that has always existed (intelligence) "was unique and separate from any other in the universe." It had strong leanings and dispositions to favor light, truth, and love and felt an innate potential to be self-directing, self-governing, and self-loving. As we came into mortality we carried with us that sense of well-being. Children have a general sense of their innate potential. But as we grow into adulthood, we as mortals begin to regularly notice what we do, how we feel, and how we feel about we do. [6] Those who have not yet reached the age of accountability are far more secure.

The Gift

I am reminded of a story told by Ester Rasband of a little boy who received a difficult assignment in school. This story teaches us that we entered mortality loving ourselves. First graders in a class were assigned to write a paper describing what they would like to be instead of themselves. The teacher thought she would receive ideas from the children such as they would rather be a lion, Spider-Man, or a firefighter. Uncharacteristically, one little boy turned in a blank paper and said to his teacher, "I'm sorry, I really tried. I thought and thought the whole time, but I couldn't think of anything I'd rather be than me."[7] As an adult, can you or I still say that? We have all seen babies in front of a mirror. They adore themselves. They giggle and are delighted to see themselves. We all felt like that at one time, but as the veil of forgetfulness becomes thicker, we learn to dislike ourselves.

However, Heavenly Father's memory never lapses in his love for us. Father in Heaven does not love us because of anything we have done or anything we are, He just loves us as a free-will gift. Likewise, my love for others should not be only because I have worked at it or because of something they have done. It should also just be available. All of us have, at one time or another, bemoaned the object of some of our affections, and we may have wished at times that we could love someone else. At such times, love was a gift. Likewise, charity is a gift.

Often I assign students in my classes at Brigham Young University to write research papers on gospel subjects. Many will choose the topic of charity and miss defining charity as a gift. As I grade those papers, I use a green pen. My dear colleague Marin Mortensen taught me not to use red ink but to use green instead, because green is a color of growth. So, on most of the research papers on charity, I will cross out lines and write thoughts all over in green because many students will equate charity with service, proposing that if one serves, one has charity. I will then explain to them that although charity always involves serving, serving is an outgrowth of charity, not the essence. I write, "You can serve without having charity; I have done it on a number of occasions."

The other misconception written by my students is that if you just do this or that then you can develop charity. I will write in green, "This is not true." I then will explain, "I can no more get up in the morning and say, 'I am going to get up and work on getting prophecy today' anymore than I can say, 'I am going to get up and work on charity today.' " We cannot give charity to ourselves; it is always a gift. The word "gift" is a synonym for charity. What I write in green all over those student's papers on the Gospel topic of charity is, "Charity is a gift not an achievement." You can achieve an MBA, work for a commission, or have a nicer yard by your efforts, but you cannot achieve charity on your own.

This gift is not usually given unless asked for. Some wives have learned this same principle in their marriages. I have a few friends who were quite amazed when they married that their husbands either did not give them anything on important occasions or gave them gifts they did not want or need. For instance, one of my friends opened up an anniversary present and found a rubber raft. She had just given birth to twins and was not thrilled with the idea of taking newborns on a raft down a river. She, along with others, has learned to ask for what she desires. Likewise, charity has to be first desired and then asked for. Elder Holland reminds us,

> Mormon explicitly taught, that this love, this ability, capacity, and reciprocation we all so want, is a gift. It is "bestowed"—that is Mormon's word. It doesn't come without effort and it doesn't come without patience but, like salvation itself, in the end it is a gift, given by God to the "true followers of his Son Jesus, Christ." The solutions to life's problems are always Gospel solutions. Not only are answers found in Christ, but so is the power, the gift, the bestowal, the miracle of giving and receiving those answers.[8]

Moroni, who recorded his father's message, was a great man who not only ran out of ore at the end of his life but also ran out of family, friends, society, civilization, and, for most part, the love of others. Gratefully, it is Moroni who teaches us how to get through any running-out-of process. Many of us will experience a diminishing of love in this dispensation of both the fulness of the gospel and the fullness of evil. Mormon teaches his son how one can love in a very frightening place where love is a rare commodity:

Wherefore my beloved brethren if ye have not charity ye are nothing, for charity never faileth. Wherefore, cleave unto charity, which is the greatest gift of all, for all things must fail—

But charity is the pure love of Christ, and it endureth forever; and whoso is found possessed of it at the last day, it shall be well with him.

Wherefore, my beloved brethren, pray unto the father with all the energy of heart, that ye may be filled with this love, which he hath bestowed upon all who are true followers of his Son, Jesus Christ; that ye may become the sons of God; that when he shall appear we shall be like him, for we shall see him as he is; that we may have this hope; that we may be purified even as he is pure. (Moroni 7:46–48)

As Mormon teaches, the Lord bestows charity on us according to our desires. Charity is not something we develop. Rather, charity is a gift that comes through earnest supplication.

When this gift is bestowed and accepted, all of our natural human tendencies are transformed, and we begin to relate to others in new ways. Charity is truly the gift that keeps giving, growing, and building over time. Mormon tells us that when we possess charity, it is a starting point to become even as the Savior. "When he shall appear we shall be like him, for we shall see him as he is" (Moroni 7:48). With charity, we will have an eternal personality and a celestial self-esteem, because when charity is received, it energizes, empowers, and eliminates the natural man. Approaches to love other than charity are flawed. Charity never fails. We can fail charity, but charity never fails us. Many gifts will be obsolete in the celestial kingdom, but charity, love, and loving, sealed relationships will not fail (1 Corinthians 13:8).

Just as there are those we enjoy giving gifts to, we can assume there may be some of our Father in Heaven's children that He is more anxious to give the gift of charity to than others. I have some friends whom I like to give gifts to and others whom I find it difficult to give to. For instance, I have one friend who, when I give her something, goes on and on about it. If I give her clothing, she will tell me it is just what she wanted and she will purposely wear it when I am with her.

For weeks she will tell me how much she enjoyed whatever I gave her. She often tells me, "You are the best gift giver and give the best things. Your presents are perfect." I love to buy things for her. Likewise, I have a little niece named Jessica who is immediately on the phone telling me how much she loves it when I mail something to her. She learned this behavior from her parents who do the same thing. I love to give to those who are appreciative.

On the other hand, I have another friend whom I struggle with when we exchange gifts. Regardless of what I give her, she never uses it, never wears it, and never mentions it. Even when I watch her while shopping and she mentions, "I want this or that" and I have gone back to the store and purchased it for her, she has not liked it. I always think when I give her something that she can get better things for herself than I could ever give her.

To what type of receiver do you think the Lord likes to give charity? If you and I want to be given charity, we need to be like my first friend. When we feel that love, or we amazingly exhibit that love to another, we too should express gratitude to our Heavenly Father, and then He will continue to bestow more of that love. Because we fail to express gratitude, most of the charity the Lord gives us may be uncollected. How valuable it would be to our emotional and mental health to examine the ways that we feel his love, experience it in our daily lives, and then express gratitude.

Instead, most of us, like spoiled children, want to dictate the way that He would give charity to us. "A loving God," our argument begins, "would surely do this or that." We then put restrictions, instructions, qualifications, and additions to the way charity is gifted. Such arguments can negate any gratitude we might express. Without this gratitude, we may fail to collect the charity, and without feeling his love, we become handicapped. His healing, energizing love is available to all. Antithetically, gratitude for God's love leads Him to give us more and more charity.

We might ask ourselves when was the last time I thanked the Lord for giving me charity? Gratitude is key to the Lord giving us this attribute. Charity is grounded, based, and rooted in a "self-abasing gratitude."[9] We could follow the example of Ester Rasband who expressed times when she experienced charity and then expressed gratitude as follows:

There are times when I'm so grateful for being loved, or so keyed in to God's love for me, that I really have it pouring out to everyone. And I think there are even some people, like my children, for instance, for whom I'm so grateful that I have love for them all the time. Anyway, I know that my love for others comes out of me—not them . . . There are also people in this ward whom I admire. But I love you whether or not I have had the opportunity to find out what I can admire in you. I thank my Heavenly Father for giving you to me to love. [10]

Jealousy: The Antonym

If one synonym for charity is gift, then to completely understand charity, we must also identify the antonym, or the emotion that cannot co-exist with charity. Much to my surprise I discovered that the opposite of love is not hate. Years ago, I heard CES speaker, Anita Canfield, at Education Week suggest that instead of hate, the antonym of charity is jealousy. In the ensuing years, the Lord has confirmed this truth to me repeatedly: Jealousy is the opposite of charity. Experiencing jealousy is experiencing charity's Anti-Christ. Therefore, to fully define charity, it is helpful to define jealousy.

The Hebrew word for jealousy "denotes an inordinate, consuming, selfish desire, arising from improper or evil motives." [11] Jealousy rears its head in a number of ways. Jealousy prevents us from sharing the good fortune of others. If we are jealous when we discover someone is happy or having a good time, we suddenly feel irritated or annoyed. Our annoyance comes from jealousy. When something good is said about someone else, we may begin to feel uncomfortable. We imagine someone else enjoying success, and we feel excluded and hurt. Jealousy has many ways of expressing itself and ways to make our lives miserable. Jealousy arises when someone else has what we are wanting. We resent that they have it and we do not. We feel them having something we want is unfair and unobtainable. Another expression of envy would be seeing a couple in love and automatically thinking that the couples' love will not last. Such a cynical attitude comes from jealousy. Envy arises when we tell ourselves that we are happy when, in reality, we are not and we want more. If I am envious of another's success, then I am wanting more success. If I am jealous because another is being loved or acknowledged, then I, too, want to be loved. Jealousy and envy reveal what we are secretly wanting but do not think we can have. Envy is a clear sign that we are denying our potential. It is one of the most agonizing of emotional states. The more we feel it, the more painful and agonizing it becomes. Unlike the healing emotions, jealousy rears its head in guilt and anger. It says you have what I want, and I am in pain because I do not have it. "Implicit in jealousy is the erroneous assumption that God is unjust, unnoticing, partial, and a respecter of persons. Jealousy can cause us to practice 'one-upmanship' or to try to manipulate family, friends, and neighbors . . . Jealousy also insists that undue importance be given to recognition, credit, applause, and to grabbing one's place in the sun, even though our insensitivity elbows others out." [12]

Jealousy partakes of pride, creating a spirit of competition that drives out the Spirit of the Lord. Moreover, in envying, we are judging something to be more important or dear to us than God or our obedience to his counsel. Brigham Young University Professor of Church history and doctrine, Brent L. Top warns, "This plague slowly robs us of spiritual strength by distracting us from the only things that will bring fulfillment and peace to our lives. "Obsession with riches . . . cankers and destroys," President Gordon B. Hinckley declared. [13] Often the cankering of the soul and the destruction of our spiritual powers that stems from materialism, greed, jealousy, and envy are so slow that we may not recognize it in ourselves until other, more serious problems appear . . . [such as having] a heart filled with covetous desires [which] has no room for the all-consuming love of God [or charity] that is required for exaltation." [14]

A heart filled with coveting requires constant reassurance; jealousy always signifies insecurity. Women and men who are jealous will feel frightened and threatened and seek to find replicas of themselves in order to feel validated. [15] That is why those without charity often feel empty like tinkling cymbals (1 Corinthians 13:1). Unfortunately, many feel this emptiness when jealousy is alive and well in families, Relief Societies, priesthood quorums, and wards. It exists everywhere.

The central feature of the jealous is enmity toward our fellow men. Enmity is defined as "hatred toward, hostility to, or a state of opposition." [16] It is the power by which Satan wishes to reign over us. Enmity tempts us daily to elevate ourselves above others and diminish them. A jealous person full of enmity pits their intellect, opinion, works, wealth, talents, or any other worldly measuring device against others. Coining the words of C. S. Lewis, "[Jealousy] gets no pleasure out of having something, only out of having more of it than the next man. . . . It is the comparison that makes you proud; the pleasure of being above the rest. Once the element of competition has gone, jealousy is gone." [17]

When we harbor jealousy, we are hard to live with because we are always uptight. Jealousy is riddled with judgment and criticism. Those dwelling in jealousy dwell in problems instead of looking for solutions. Jealousy is based not on another's actions but on our reactions to their actions. With jealousy, we are filled with competition, which is one of Satan's most effective tools for destroying relationships and crippling ease between ourselves and others. Such interpersonal competition is not, nor can be, related to righteousness. Righteousness instead comes from love or charity.

Looking at this antonym of charity helps us to understand charity. Likewise, looking at synonyms to define charity also broadens our understanding. We have already discussed that one synonym of charity is gift, a second synonym is gratitude, and a third is love. The pure love of Christ is the scriptural definition (Moroni 7:47). Enmeshed inside that pure love of Christ will also be a pure love of self, or self-esteem.

Love of Self

The correct loving of self is a difficult concept to comprehend but is understood by those possessing charity. Charity, or love, is the crux of the first and second commandments given by the Lord Jesus Christ. You will remember that the Lord was asked by a lawyer to identify the greatest commandment (Matthew 22:35–36). Christ responded by identifying the two greatest commandments rather than choosing one of the more than six hundred rules that the Pharisees lived by. Christ identified these commandments as, "Thou shalt love the Lord thy God with all thy heart, and with all thy soul, and with all thy mind. This is the first and great commandment. And the second is like unto it,

Thou shalt love thy neighbor as thyself" (Matthew 22:37–39). As Ester Rasband has noted, to love your neighbor the way you love yourself means you want no ill for him as you want none for yourself. You feel the sorrows and joys of your neighbor as you do for yourself, and you're concerned for his survival and welfare as much as you are for yourself. Though the Lord listed two admonitions, "it is common for us to read this scripture as if it actually contains three commandments:

Love God.

Love your neighbor.

Love yourself. [18]

Somehow, we mingle God's great commandments with a worldly philosophy that leads us to explore self-awareness. The world puts emphasis on "the words 'as thyself' [as if it is] an admonition to identify with others and seek their comfort as you would your own . . . The Lord did not command us to love ourselves. He simply acknowledged that we do. . . . It is a human fact that we seek our own comfort, [and] seek our own survival." [19] As the prophet David O. McKay said, "Nature's law demands us to do everything with self in view. Self-preservation is the first law of mortal life." [20]

It is the world that teaches us a false sense of self. Timothy B. Smith, a Brigham Young University Associate Professor of Psychology, has further defined what the world teaches about loving one's self:

> The world, with its emphasis on self-gratification and self-fulfillment, frequently teaches that happiness is found through a focus on self: getting in touch with ourselves, satisfying our needs, boosting our self-esteem. Books and organizations that teach about self-esteem, self-appreciation, self-respect, self-acceptance, and a host of related "self" concepts enjoy great popularity. [21]

Many of us have bought into this kind of drugstore/TV talk show/ worldly philosophy. Patricia Holland, former member of the Young Women general presidency, has observed that some Latter-day Saints have adapted,

> The feminist books, the talk show hosts, or the whole media culture to sell us a bill of goods—or rather a

bill of no goods. We can become so sidetracked in our compulsive search for identity and self-esteem that we really believe it can be found in having perfect figures or academic degrees or professional status or even absolute motherly success. . . . We often worry so much about pleasing and performing for others that we lose our uniqueness—that full and relaxed acceptance of one's self as a person of worth and individuality. We become so frightened and insecure that we cannot be generous toward the diversity and individuality, and yes, problems, of our neighbors. Too many women with these anxieties watch helplessly as their lives unravel from the very core that centers and sustains them.

Too many of us are struggling and suffering, too many are running faster than they have strength, expecting too much of themselves. As a result, we are experiencing new and undiagnosed stress-related illnesses. The Epstein–Barr virus, for one, has come into our popular medical jargon. . . . "[The victims] are plagued by low-grade fevers, aching joints, and sometimes a sore throat—but they don't have the flu. They're overwhelmingly exhausted, weak, and debilitated—but they don't have AIDS. They're often confused and forgetful—but it isn't Alzheimer's. Many patients feel suicidal, but it isn't clinical depression. . . . Female victims outnumber males about 3 to 1, and a great many are intelligent high achievers with stressful lives."

Surely there has not been another time in history when women have questioned their self-worth as harshly and critically as in the second half of the twentieth century. Many women are searching, almost frantically, as never before, for a sense of personal purpose and meaning; and many LDS women are searching, too, for eternal insight and meaning in their femaleness.

If I were Satan and wanted to destroy a society, I think I would stage a full-blown blitz on women. I would keep them so distraught and distracted that they would never find the calming strength and serenity for which their sex has always been known.

Satan has effectively done that, catching us in the crunch of trying to be superhuman instead of striving to reach our unique, God-given potential within such diversity. He tauntingly teases us that if we don't have it all—fame, fortune, families, and fun, and have it all the time—we have been shortchanged and are second-class citizens in the race of life. As a sex we are struggling, our families are struggling, and our society is struggling. [22]

With Elder Jeffrey R. Holland, Sister Holland further queried,

Too many are like a ship at sea without sail or rudder, "tossed to and fro," as the Apostle Paul said (see Ephesians 4:14), until more and more of us are genuinely, rail-grabbingly seasick.

Where is the sureness that allows us to sail our ship whatever winds may blow, with the master seaman's triumphant cry, "Steady as she goes"? Where is the inner stillness we so cherish and for which women have traditionally been known? [23]

As outlined above, the world's answer to our struggles is to concentrate on self. Modern terms overemphasize self and distort the nature of our existence and the purpose of life. The Lord's answer is to lose ourselves in others through charity. The world teaches that we are separate entities. The scriptures teach that we are spiritually and socially connected. Exaltation is not offered to individuals in isolation from others, rather exaltation requires the bonds of eternal marriage. It also requires dedication to those around us. Those who have little connection with others or who have not learned the importance of relationships face the egocentric pull of selfishness. President Ezra Taft Benson called "selfishness one of the common faces of pride . . . [that leads to] self-conceit, self-pity, worldly self-fulfillment, self-gratification and self-seeking." [24] And the distance between constant self-pleasing and self-worship is shorter than we think.

If we can turn away from the physical preoccupations, super-woman and superman accomplishments, and endless popularity contests, and return instead to the wholeness of our souls, that unity in our very being that balances the demanding and inevitable diversity of life, we will experience charity. To truly find ourselves, we must lose ourselves, and the only way to do that is to ask the Savior to bestow upon us the gift of charity.

1. Jeffrey R. Holland, "How do I Love Thee?" *Brigham Young University Speeches 1999–2000,* (Provo: Brigham Young University Publications & Graphics, 2000), 158.

2. Virginia H. Pearce, ed., *Glimpses into the Life and Heart of Marjorie Pay Hinckley,* (Salt Lake City: Deseret Book, 1999), 59.

3. Russell M. Nelson, "Divine Love," *Ensign,* February 2003, 20.

4. Ester Rasband, *Confronting the Myth of Self-Esteem: Twelve Keys to Finding Peace* (Salt Lake City: Deseret Book, 1998), 51 and 54.

5. Bryan Forbes, Robert B. Sherman, Richard M. Sherman, Angela Morley (Musical Direction/Supervision, Musical Arrangement), "The Slipper and the Rose," *Image Entertainment,* http://movies2.nytimes.com/gst/movies/movie.html?v_id=129046, accessed 2 October 2001.

6. Richard L. Bednar and Scott R. Peterson, *Spirituality and Self-Esteem: Developing the Inner Self* (Salt Lake City: Deseret Book, 1990), 11–12.

7. Ester Rasband, *Confronting the Myth of Self-Esteem: Twelve Keys to Finding Peace* (Salt Lake City: Deseret Book, 1998), 49–50.

8. Jeffrey R. Holland, "How Do I Love Thee?" *Brigham Young University Speeches 1999–2000,* (Provo: Brigham Young University Publications & Graphics, 2000), 158.

9. Ester Rasband, *Confronting the Myth of Self-Esteem: Twelve Keys to Finding Peace* (Salt Lake City: Deseret Book, 1998), 62–63.

10. Ibid., 55.

11. Brent L. Top, "'Thou Shalt Not Covet'," *Ensign*, December 1994, 22.

12. Neal A. Maxwell, *Lord, Increase Our Faith* (Salt Lake City: Deseret Book, 1994), 98.

13. Gordon B. Hinckley, "First Presidency Message 'Thou Shalt Not Covet,'" *Ensign*, March 1990, 5.

14. Brent L. Top, "'Thou Shalt Not Covet'," *Ensign*, December 1994, 24–25.

15. Patricia T. Holland, "'One Thing Needful': Becoming Women of Greater Faith in Christ," *Ensign*, October 1987, 29.

16. Ezra Taft Benson, "Beware of Pride," *Ensign*, May 1989, 4.

17. C. S. Lewis, *Mere Christianity*, (New York: Macmillan, 1952), 110.

18. Ester Rasband, *Confronting the Myth of Self-Esteem: Twelve Keys to Finding Peace* (Salt Lake City: Deseret Book, 1998), 71 and 69.

19. Ibid., 71–73.

20. David O. McKay, *Conference Report*, April 1957, 7.

21. Timothy B. Smith, "I Have a Question," *Ensign*, September 1999, 59.

22. Patricia T. Holland, "'One Thing Needful': Becoming Women of Greater Faith in Christ," *Ensign*, Oct. 1987, 26–34. See also "The Puzzling Virus," *Newsweek*, 27 October 1986:105.

23. Jeffery R. Holland and Patricia T. Holland, *On Earth As It Is in Heaven* (Salt Lake City: Deseret Book, 1998), 86.

24. Ezra Taft Benson, "Beware of Pride," *Ensign*, May 1989, 6.

Chapter 7
The Charitable Qualities

As we receive the gift of charity, Satan will attempt to block any increased efforts to love God or our neighbors. Especially, throughout the last century, Satan has enticed all humanity to engage almost all of their energies in the pursuit of romantic love, thing-love, or excessive self-love, instead of the pure love of Christ. Paying attention to Satan's counterfeit, we sometimes forget that appropriate self-love and self-esteem are promised rewards for putting others first. Christ promised: "Whosoever shall seek to save his life shall lose it: and whosoever shall lose his life shall preserve it" (Luke 17:33). President Kimball explained: "We become more substantive as we serve others—indeed, it is easier to 'find' ourselves because there is so much more of us to find!"[1] As our souls progress, we pay less attention to praise and care little about public disapproval, becoming free to be ourselves and free to love others. A desire to serve others comes directly from the gift of charity.

Charity, or the pure love of Christ, initiates and sustains all other spiritual qualities. President Brigham Young informed Latter-day Saints: "There is one virtue, attribute, or principle, which, if cherished and practised by the Saints, would prove salvation to thousands upon thousands. I allude to charity, or love, from which proceed forgiveness, long-suffering, kindness, and patience."[2]

These attributes and personality characteristics Brigham Young lists above are sometimes mistaken for charity. They are not the gift, rather, they are the result of the possession of the gift. Those who possess such qualities are displaying charity. The opportunity to develop these charitable characteristics is open to all whereas other attributes are not always available. As Elder Jeffery R. Holland suggests:

> There are lots of limitations in all of us that we hope [others] will overlook. I suppose no one is as handsome or as beautiful as he or she wishes or as brilliant in school or as witty in speech or as wealthy as we would like but in a world of varied talents and fortunes that we can't always command, I think that makes even more attractive the qualities we can command such qualities as thoughtfulness, patience, a kind word, and true delight in the accomplishment of another. These cost us nothing, and they can mean everything to the one who receives them. [3]

Numerous verses in the scriptures describe the same cluster of spiritual qualities Elder Holland talks about above. The Old Testament describes them in Exodus 34; in the Book of Mormon King Benjamin lists them in Mosiah 3; the Doctrine and Covenants describes them to priesthood leaders in section 121; Paul describes them to the Corinthians; and Moroni finishes his record by talking about them in Moroni 10. Whereas the attributes of wit, beauty, or wealth are optional for eternal self-worth, the charitable qualities are not. They must be part and parcel of our eternal personalities and our celestial self-esteem. They are the very qualities prerequisite for Godhood. Joseph Smith warned, "If you wish to go where God is, you must be like God, or possess the principles which God possesses." [4] The charitable qualities become the litmus test for a celestial state.

Behavioral scientists have developed many personality tests. Among such tests is a color code that has defined personalities according to four colors. [5] After studying "the color code," I heard someone say, "Well, I am a red, so I guess that's why I'm bossy." Another suggested, "I'm just a yellow, so boy, am I fun, but I'm not very responsible." I ask both of these individuals, "What color or personality do you think Jesus Christ is?" Though you may be a red, yellow, or whatever other modern label you may use to describe yourself, the true label of self-esteem is to become like him. His key personality characteristic is enmeshed in his pure love.

As we look at the traits displayed by one possessing charity, we must continue to remember these characteristics are not something we develop; rather, they are the fruits of charity. Many of us seek these fruits of charity, yet find them to be elusive in our daily lives. The problem in daily life is we do not know what is going to happen on any given day. For instance, I do not know if an inept sales clerk at a store is going to push my patience, or if someone will pull out in front of my car and I will become irritated. Our response to such situations should be to get on our knees and beg the Lord for charity each morning, and then the Lord through the Holy Ghost will help us face things with charity come what may. At the end of a day when we have been blessed with the gift of charity, we might think to ourselves, "My goodness, when that salesclerk kept me in line for twenty-five minutes and charged my credit card three times, I was patient. Heavenly Father, thank you for bestowing thy gift on me today." Then we will remember those traits were not developed by our own efforts; rather, we displayed the fruits of charity given by a loving Heavenly Father. Scripturally some of these characteristics or fruits of charity are hard to define and conceptualize. Elder Neal A. Maxwell produced a list of antonyms and synonyms for each characteristic found in Moroni 10 that helps us to more clearly identify those possessing charity.[6] We will list each characteristic by describing what we are to be and what we are not to be as follows:

We Are to Be:	We Are Not to Be:
Meek and Humble	*Self-concerned, dismissive, proud, seeking ascendancy*

Many associate the word meekness with weakness. Meekness and weakness are not synonyms. The Savior was the epitome of meekness, but He was never weak. As Bednar and Peterson declare, "Humility originates in personal strength, not in weakness. Humility is not self-abasement, servile, submissiveness, or devaluing ourselves, as so many seem to believe. Rather, it is doing our very best and then quietly leaving our acts, expressions, and accomplishments to speak for themselves. Humility is a strength, a power within those who quietly and unpretentiously have been moved by the Holy Spirit."[7] Elder Maxwell's definition of this characteristic is enlightening. He teaches that meekness "is more than self-restraint; it is the presentation of self in a posture of kindness and gentleness, reflecting certitude, strength, serenity, and a healthy self-esteem and self-control."[8] That control comes from certain attitudes that the gift of charity ensues.

With charity the very wording of our thoughts produces adjustments in our self-esteem. For instance, if we want to increase a little child's self-esteem, the world would teach us to say to him when something goes awry: "Don't worry; you're wonderful." A better phrase instead would be "Don't worry about being wonderful."[9] The world would suggest we also cultivate this attitude in ourselves and children, "You've got to feel good about yourself" or "You're special just the way you are." Such a stance fits in with the popular saying, "I've gotta be me." The world also incorrectly teaches that being meek is to think, "I'm a nobody." We sometimes think of someone who is humble as insecure. Instead, Christian philosopher C. S. Lewis describes what it is like to meet a meek man in his work *Mere Christianity* as follows:

> We must not think pride is something God forbids because He is offended at it, or that humility is something He demands as due to His own dignity—as if God Himself was proud. He is not in the least worried about His dignity. The point is, He wants you to know Him: wants to give you Himself. And He and you are two things of such a kind that if you really get into any kind of touch with Him you will, in fact, be humble—delightedly humble, feeling the infinite relief of having for once got rid of all the silly nonsense about your own dignity which has made you restless and unhappy all your life. He is trying to make you humble in order to make this moment possible: trying to take off a lot of silly, ugly, fancy-dress in which we have all got ourselves up and are strutting about like the little idiots we are. I wish I had got a bit of further with humility myself: if I had, I could probably tell you more about the relief, the comfort, of taking the fancy-dress off—getting rid of the false self, with all its "Look at me" and "Aren't I a good boy?" and all its posing and posturing. To get even near it, even for a moment, is like a drink of cold water to a man in a desert.[10]

As Lewis describes, possessing humility and meekness is not thinking we are nothing, no good, or lower than others. Instead, humility and meekness comes in our comparison to our Savior and our Father in Heaven. "When Moses observed after [his] revelatory vision that 'man is nothing,' this surely was not a reflection on man, 'God's greatest miracle,' but a placing of man in the vast perspective of God's creations and a realizing, even so, that we are God's exclusive work and his greatest glory." [11]

Most problems linked with a low self-image or feelings of unworthiness, are the result of a false view of how God sees us. If we can learn to bring our self-image in harmony with the Lord's view of us then we will be empowered to change our negative thoughts and eventually change our negative behaviors.

Humility is the acknowledged dependence on our Father in Heaven's love that will lead us to charity. [12] When Moroni says, "If ye have not charity, ye are nothing" (Moroni 7:46), I do not believe he meant we are worthless. Even the most vile, wicked human being is valued of the Lord: "the worth of souls is great in the sight of God" (D&C 18:10). Instead, I believe Moroni implies that if you do not have charity and only think about yourself, you will *feel* like nothing. Lewis enlightened this concept when he stated, "The real test of being in the presence of God is that you either forget about yourself altogether or see yourself as a small, dirty object. It is better to forget about yourself altogether." [13]

Meekness is not being proud or self-concerned. Indeed the false display of humility or the world's counterfeit of this produces the antithesis of a humble person. The most self-concerned people are sometimes those who are full of self-pity. The attitude of "woe is me" leaves little room to think of others. "How many neighbors go unloved because people first despise themselves?" [14]

In short, those who are humble seldom think about themselves at all. President Spencer W. Kimball explains, "Humility is teachableness—an ability to realize that all virtues and abilities are not concentrated in one's self. . . . Humility is gracious, quiet, serene— not pompous, spectacular, not histrionic. It is subdued, kindly, and understanding. . . . It never struts nor swaggers. [Humility is] faithful, quiet works. . . . Humility is repentant. . . it is the doing of one's best in every case and leaving one's acts, expressions, and accomplishments to largely speak for themselves." [15] In describing such meekness Paul uses another image describing the meek as those who are not "puffed up." Illuminating this image, Elder Holland asked: "Haven't you ever been with someone who was so conceited, so full of themselves that they seemed like the Pillsbury Dough boy?" You know the kind; "such a fellow walk[s] down Lover's Lane holding his own hand. True love, [in fact, all love] blooms when we care more about another person than we care about ourselves." [16] If we are to teach our children meekness and humility, we do not stress "You are capable and lovable"; instead we emphasize, "You are loved and grateful." [17] We stress not that we are special but we are special to Jesus Christ. Such attitudes are encircled in the gift of charity.

We Are to Be:	We Are Not to Be:
Patient	*Hectic, hurried, pushy, . . . intolerant of ineptness*

Patience is really a gift for me. I am not a naturally patient, deliberate, or slow person. As a little girl I always bit into the Tootsie Roll Pop. Still, I never just lick ice cream cones, I gulp them down. I am at my worst in long lines. My natural tendency is to be pushy and most of the time I am hectic and hurried. My behavior is characteristic of our fast-paced society. That is not the way of charity. We cannot have charity without also being patient. In my life when I feel great patience, I know I am experiencing one of the fruits of charity as a gift from my Heavenly Father. God constantly reinforces the principle of patience in our lives. President Joseph F. Smith observed:

> God's ways of educating our desires are, of course, always the most perfect. . . . And what is God's way? Everywhere in nature we are taught the lessons of patience and waiting. We want things a long time before we get them, and the fact that we wanted them a long time makes them all the more precious when they come. In nature we have our seedtime and harvest; and if children were taught that the desires that they sow may be reaped by and by through patience and labor, they will learn to appreciate whenever a

long-looked-for goal has been reached. Nature resists us and keeps admonishing us to wait; indeed, we are compelled to wait. [18]

Patience produces a Latter-day Saint who is, as Paul told the Ephesians, "rooted and grounded in love" (Ephesians 3:17). Charity enables us "to comprehend with all saints what is the breadth, and length, and depth, and height; And to know the love of Christ, which passeth knowledge, that ye might be filled with all the fulness of God" or Godly patience (Ephesians 3:18–19). Patience becomes important in some of our life's path as it "helps us to realize that while we may be ready to move on, having had enough of a particular learning experience, our continuing presence is often a needed part of the learning environment of others." [19] Discipleship is not a hectic thing, and it usually causes more calm, peace, and trust in God's tutoring of each of us even when things are unfair. [20] Indeed, patience brings blessings to those who are willing to wait.

One of my favorite stories about this fruit of charity is told by Elder Dean Larsen of the Quorum of the First Seventy,

> There is the story of two neighboring farmers—one a habitual Sabbath breaker, and the other a faithful observer of the Lord's day. On one occasion the Sabbath observer severely chastised his neighbor for working his farm on Sundays rather than attending to his religious devotions. This led to an argument and a challenge. "Let us put the matter to a test," the Sabbath breaker said. "We will select two pieces of ground of equal size and fertility. On them we will plant the same crop. My piece of ground I will work on Sundays, and you will work yours on the other days of the week. Then we will see who gets the greater harvest."
>
> The challenge was accepted and the conditions were faithfully observed. As the harvest was gathered in, the Sabbath-observing farmer was disappointed to learn that the piece of ground farmed by his neighbor had produced the greater yield. The Sabbath breaker exulted in his apparent triumph and his discrediting of the contention of his faithful neighbor.

"You have forgotten one important thing," protested the Sabbath-observer. "The Lord doesn't always settle his accounts in October." [21]

Patience allows us to remember that the Lord does not always settle His accounts in October or this year or maybe even in this moral existence, but He does settle them. Having such an attitude is one of the gifts of charity, and such an attitude produces a relaxation that releases us from some of our natural tendencies towards being hectic, hurried, pushy, or intolerant.

We Are to Be:	**We Are Not to Be:**
Full of love	*Demanding, dominating, harsh, manipulative, condescending* [22]

According to Elder Maxwell, one who is full of love is not demanding, dominating, harsh, manipulative or condescending. Those who are full of love do not send messages to others that display any of these negative behaviors. In juxtaposition, one full of charity supplies moments of needed response. "The smile of one friend is like a standing ovation. A compliment can part the curtain on their unappreciated possibilities." [23]

Satan's counterfeits of being full of love are being executed in a precision as the world has never before seen. One of his counterfeits is to be full of lust, rather than being full of love. A few years ago, I visited Denmark where acceptance of the Gospel is substantially diminishing. When I asked one mission president why this trend was developing, he made this observation: "It is no wonder conversions are difficult. Since 1970 when pornography was legalized, Satan has filled the very air with pornography and the gospel of Jesus Christ has a hard time permeating such pollution." Our airwaves are also being cluttered with lust. Recently, a dear friend of mine was appalled at a shoe commercial which aired showing two young men involved in an immoral act. It violated her home as it came across the screen during an appropriate family program. She contacted the shoe company, called the television station, and wrote letters asking that the commercial be deleted from family programs. Such actions were an outgrowth of her being full of love. Elder Maxwell warned: "More than we know, the alienation abroad in the land is due in significant measure to the gross sexual immorality—before which faith, hope, and charity all fall. That special triad of virtues is savaged by unchastity."[24]

We Are to Be:	We Are Not to Be:
Gentle	*Coarse, brusque, vindictive*

One full of love is also one who is gentle. Modern society sometimes produces men and women who are the opposite of gentleness. The world's ever pressing philosophies has produced both males and females who are devoid of love or charity. Elder Maxwell explains, "Along with the traditional, predatory, selfish male there is now the predatory, selfish female. Both, driven by appetite, have a false sense of being free—but it is, alas, the same sort of empty freedom." Observing one such person, the English philosopher William Law, in writing of a lady of some renown, said that she was "nice in everything that concerned her body or dress, careless of everything that might benefit her soul."[25]

The most gentle of all who walked the earth was our Savior. President John Taylor characterized Gentle Jesus this way: "The Savior acts not as a foolish, vindictive man, to knock another man down. He is full of kindness, long suffering, and forbearance, and treats everybody with kindness and courtesy."[26] Likewise, Elder Jeffrey R. Holland observes, "In all that Christ was, He was not ever envious or inflated, never consumed with His own needs. He did not once, not ever, seek His own advantage at the expense of someone else. He delighted in the happiness of others, the happiness He could bring them. He was forever kind."[27]

We can tell if we are becoming gentle like the Savior by asking ourselves some questions. Are we gentle when we are irritated? Can we reach out to help others even when we are beset with personal problems? How good are we at receiving bad news? What kind of a car driver are we? Elder Maxwell observed, "Sensitive and defensive driving protects riders in both cars when a foot is removed from the accelerator of ego. Irritability indicates that one feels imposed upon."[28] If we exhibit irritability over doing these daily things, it betrays "a lack of gentleness."

Gentleness is vital, especially in marital relationships. Elder Jeffrey R. Holland explains the necessity for gentleness in romantic relationships:

> Love is a fragile thing, and some elements in life can try to break it. Much damage can be done if we are not in tender hands, caring hands. To give ourselves totally to another person, as we do in marriage, is the most trusting step we take in any human relationship. . . . If we do it right we end up sharing everything—all our hopes, all our fears, all our dreams, all our weaknesses, and all our joys—with another person.
>
> In the spirit of Mormon's plea for pure love, I want to impress upon you the vulnerability and delicacy of your partner's future as it is placed in your hands for safekeeping—male and female, it works both ways. [29]

Elder Holland is one who has personally learned the art of gentleness. He describes his approach with his wife as follows, "I know . . . clearly how to help [Pat] and, if I let myself, I know exactly what will hurt her . . . To impair or impede her in any way for my gain or vanity or emotional mastery over her should disqualify me on the spot to be her husband. Indeed, it should consign my miserable soul to eternal incarceration in that large and spacious building." [30]

Elder Holland warned:

> In a dating and courtship relationship, I would not have you spend five minutes with someone who belittles you, who is constantly critical of you, who is cruel at your expense and may even call it humor. Life is tough enough without having the person who is supposed to love you leading the assault on your self-esteem, your sense of dignity, your confidence, and your joy. In this person's care you deserve to feel physically and emotionally secure. . . . Find someone who brings out the best in you and is not envious of your success. Find someone who suffers when you suffer and who finds his or her happiness in your own.
>
> Temper tantrums are not cute even in children; they are despicable in adults, especially adults who are

supposed to love each other. We are too easily provoked; we are too inclined to think that our partner meant to hurt us—meant to do us evil, so to speak; and in defensive or jealous response we too often rejoice when we see them make a mistake and find them in a fault. Let's show some discipline on this one. Act a little more maturely. [31]

As Elder Holland described, the maturity of charity is exhibited in gentleness. Likewise, poet William Wordsworth observed, "That best portion of a good man's life; his little, nameless, unremembered acts of kindness and of love." [32]

We Are to Be:	We Are Not to Be:
Easily entreated	*Unapproachable, inaccessible, non-listening, and stereotyping of others*

To entreat means to ask earnestly or to implore. A person who is easily entreated asks people about themselves and implores to gain knowledge about others. We want to be around such a person because it is easy to open up to them. Being easily entreated cuts down on verbalism. How can we become like our Father in Heaven and Savior if we are poor listeners? And listening includes hearing others who are logistically down or sideways to us as well as above. That listening includes even listening to children. I am reminded of a mother who was easily entreated by a child, listened, was approachable and accessible, and it greatly blessed her family. Dan and Nan Barker in Arizona had been blessed to adopt four children.

> Some time ago, Nate, then just over three said: "Mommy, there is another little girl who is supposed to come to our family. She has dark hair and dark eyes and she lives a long way from here."
>
> The wise mother asked, "How do you know this?"
>
> To which her son replied: "Jesus told me, upstairs."

The Baker home did not have an upstairs. Nan was easily entreated. She listened to her son, got in touch with an international adoption agency, and the Barkers were eventually sealed in the Salt Lake Temple to a little girl with dark hair and dark eyes. [33]

I too had a wonderful experience being taught to be easily entreated by a child. After I had a heart breaking experience, my five-year-old nephew quoted a country song to me. He said, "Aunt Mary Jane do you know what happens when you fall in love?" I replied, "Not lately." He said, "Well you lose your heart." I then asked him, "Then what happens, Brock?" He answered, "Well Jesus puts it back again. And it is a miracle." When Jesus puts our hearts back again it is miraculous! Such a blessing of having our hearts put back again is a fruit of being easily entreated.

"Many of us do what Jesus never did: we talk too much." [34] Brigham Young said, "You cannot hide the heart, when the mouth is open." [35] Those who are easily entreated do not participate in the multiplying of words. On the other hand, Elder Maxwell tells us that those of us who multiply words are usually displaying "a desire for more air time." Those who are easily entreated are "more settled in their views; they can be succinct without feeling unappreciated. They can even let someone else say what they would have said and still not feel left out." [36]

A good barometer for the characteristic of being easily entreated is to ask ourselves, "What kind of a friend am I?" Do I have to be heard all the time? Do I pause in conversations? Such listeners are rare in our modern society. One woman told me she had many first dates where she could count the number of sentences on one hand that she had said and yet learned the man's entire life story in one evening. Another complained to me of the telephone calls she had with other women for what seemed like hours and all she contributed was, "uh-huh." I would suggest we look at our relationships and ask ourselves how much does the other person know about me and how much do I know about them? If those tallies are lopsided we need to take some action and pray for the charity that helps us take a real interest in others.

Charity involves finding, focusing, and nurturing the positive in others along with listening.

We Are to Be:	We Are Not to Be:
Long-suffering	*Impatient, disinterested, curt, easily offended [and unable to endure]*

Long-suffering is acknowledging that God knows what we are passing through. Through his foreknowledge he already knows the outcome of that passing through and has taken our actions into account along with others' actions. President David O. McKay makes a wonderful promise that our hopes for the things that really matter will not be held at bay by others or circumstances.

> We may "rough-hew our ends"; we may choose our course; but God will overrule our acts and the acts of nations for the consummation of his divine purposes.

> God is standing in the shadow of eternity, it seems to me, deploring now the inevitable results of the follies, the transgressions, and the sins of his wayward children, but we cannot blame him for these any more than we can blame a father who might say to his son: "There are two roads, my son, one leading to the right, one leading to the left. If you take the one to the right, it will lead you to success and happiness. If you take the one to the left, it will bring upon you misery and unhappiness, and perhaps death, but you choose which you will. You must choose: I will not force either upon you."

> The young man starts out and, seeing the allurements and the attractiveness of the road to the left, and thinking it is a short cut to his happiness, he concludes to take it. The father knows what will become of him. He knows that not far from that flowery path there is a mire-hole into which his boy will fall; he knows that after he struggles out of that mire-hole he will come to a slough into which he will flounder. He sees others who have chosen that path in that same slough,

and he knows that in their struggle to get on dry land
there will be fighting. He could see it long before the
boy reached that condition, and he could, therefore,
foretell it. The father loves the boy just the same and
would still continue to warn him and plead for him to
return to the right path.

God, too, has shown the world, through his prophets
in ages gone by, that many of his people, individuals
as well as nations, would choose the path that leads to
misery and death, and he foretold it, but the responsibility is upon those who would not heed God's
message, not upon God. But in his infinite wisdom,
he will overrule these transgressors for the good of
all his sons and daughters. His love for them is always
manifested. [37]

And as President McKay further instructs, sometimes God will
intervene and bring better things than we had even hoped for: "I have
a faith in the overruling power of Providence. . . . A wise Father will
work out of men's mistakes and blunders greater blessings than they
might have obtained with their own wisest foresight." [38] Therefore,
as Joseph Smith told us, God "has made ample provision." [39] Long-
suffering, endurance, and patience are all designed to be the constant
companions of charity. Constancy is a fruit of charity, hence there is
no such thing as bursts of long-suffering.

Sometimes such long-suffering may be misread as a weakness by
others. And sometimes when we are suffering long instead of enduring
it well, we pass suffering on to others. If we become overcome with
self-pity, we simply ignore others by saying in effect "I have all I can
handle with my own problems." Jesus was never involved in self-pity.
"Even while Jesus was literally providing salvation for all mankind, the
perfect Shepherd simultaneously reached out to individuals." [40]

Part of the "pressing forward" that Nephi talks of is taking others
with us (2 Nephi 31:20). Or if they will not come along, if they misrep-
resent, misquote, or misuse us part of that long suffering is also praying
sincerely for those who despitefully use us. Such prayers are examples
of long-suffering. Those suffering long are a blessing to others as Elder
Holland says in the following:

Some things in life we have little or no control over. These have to be endured. Some disappointments have to be lived with [even] in love and marriage. . . . We have to hope for an end to such sorrows and difficulty, we have to endure until things come right in the end. . . . No one ought to have to face such trials alone. We can endure almost anything if we have someone at our side who truly loves us, who is easing our burden and lightening our load. [41]

The perfect pattern of long-suffering is our Father in Heaven. I am so grateful that He does not become bored with the same old plan or get people fatigue or even Mary Jane fatigue.

We Are to Be:
Submissive

We Are Not to Be:
Resistant to the Spirit, life's lessons and instructive feedback, and unwilling to endure

Those who are submissive are not at the mercy of others or of circumstances. If we can utter the words "It is alright" or "It will be OK" even when we are confronted with things we cannot fully understand, then we will know that God is still in charge. When we truly want God's will more than our own, then his guidance is much more available to us. Some may accuse those who submit in such a way of having no courage or backbone. In reality, submitting is a most courageous course of action. The Book of Mormon calls this characteristic being swallowed up in the will of the Father (Mosiah 15:7) In similar fashion, one of the legacies of Elder Maxwell is to remind us that, "The submission of one's will is really the only uniquely personal thing we have to place on God's altar." [42]

With submission, we become more willing to learn from the Spirit and from life's lessons, even seeing at times some disappointments as blessings in disguise. I am reminded of a situation a few years ago when, because of a supervisor's lack of integrity, seven employees made the decision to leave employment where they had all devoted themselves and built programs. Most were ill treated and misrepresented. It was disappointing to say the least. Amazingly, out of that experience all seven of those employees ended up in much better situations. One employee was terminated after seventeen years of service. There was no gold watch, not even a pat on the back. He was sorely disappointed, but as he stood for what he felt was right and tried to follow the Spirit even though he had no idea where he would find employment, the Lord guided and directed him to a much better future career.

A blessing in disguise was also experienced by sailors on the port bound *U. S. S. Enterprise.* The *Enterprise* was slowed by heavy seas and a malfunctioning escort destroyer, the *U. S. S. Dunlap.* Hence, the *Enterprise* did not make it to its destination of Pearl Harbor as scheduled for the weekend of 7 December 1941. However, eighteen planes were permitted to take off and proceed to Hawaii. Some left behind on the ship must have envied those lucky pilots. However, those unfortunate planes arrived during the attack of Pearl Harbor and six were shot down.[43] Handling our disappointments with long-suffering may bring us unforeseen blessings also.

We Are to Be:

Temperate (self-restrained)

We Are Not to Be:

Egoistic, eager for attention and recognition, and too talkative

When I think of the word temperate, I also think of the word balance. Satan seeks to bring imbalance into our lives. He is so clever he can even take our good traits and turn them to our disadvantage. This quote by Church educator Bryant S. Hinckley explains how imbalance can undermine our strengths:

> If we are over enthusiastic, our enthusiasm may become fanaticism. If we are strongly emotional, our emotion may lead to hysterics. If we are excessively imaginative. . . . We may become visionary and flighty. . . . If we have a superabundance of courage, it may manifest itself in recklessness. . . . If we are super-sympathetic, our sympathy can become weakness and run into sentimentalism, if we are original, our originality may become an eccentricity. Piety may become sanctimoniousness. And every virtue may

become a vice—every grace a defect. It is the balance
of these virtues that makes the strong man. [44]

Being temperate keeps our gifts in balance. A temperate person
also acts; they do not react. As marriage and family therapist Garth L.
Allred puts it, they do not over-react or under-react.

Under-reacting and over-reacting are the world's counterfeit of
the qualities of charity. For instance, someone who wants to be gentle
may under-react. Fearing they may not be tender enough or loving
enough, they become pleasers, weak, inhibited, withdrawn and shy,
trying to please everyone but themselves. Trying to please everyone
is a prefect formula for failure. Clinging to negative thoughts such as
feelings of loneliness and detachment, those who are intemperate and
under-react may feel being loved by someone is more important than
being respected. Such people who lack charity will stay in unhealthy
relationships much longer than is wise or expedient. Lyrics like "As
Long as He Needs Me" and "Stand By Your Man" are their theme
songs. They stay in unhealthy relationships at all costs even if it means
submitting themselves to extreme abuse and act as enablers for people
who over-react, which is another face of intemperance. [45]

Over-reactors participate in the fight-or-flight response to stress.
Emotion generated by the flight response is fear and related to feelings of anxiety, timidity, shyness, inhibition, reticence, apprehen-
sion, and even terror. Without charity and temperance, over-reactors
run away rather than stand their ground. People who over-react are
involved in great cover-ups. They may feel unworthy or lonely, so they
pretend to be very confidant or egotistic. Allred describes over-reactors
in the following way, "They assume an air of self-confidence and an
overbearing manner that is obnoxious and arrogant. They nurse their
wrath to keep it warm so they can dump their anger on anyone who
disagrees with them. They always want to engage in a fight. They
refuse suggestions from those who want to help." [46] Criticism is unac-
ceptable to over-reactors because in their mind it diminishes them
in some way. They need heavy doses of recognition, acting out the
role of superiority to compensate for their unworthy feelings. They
intimidate people into conforming to their expectations. They need
power and control. According to Allred, "other emotions associated
with overreacting are hostility, resentment, guilt (anger at oneself),
rage, seething, depression, and hurt. . . . being mean, vulgar, rude,

aggressive, and abusive." Those who over-react rank themselves and others according to position. They are controlling in their relationships and seek out those they can manipulate and control. Over-reacting is a false form of being strong. Fearing they will be seen as weak, some people over-react, becoming mean, vicious, crude, abusive. In fits of anger, abusers think that they are gaining victory, while at the same time the victims of such abuse submit to the evil in martyr-like ways. They think they are pleasing God by not resisting the abuse, or they falsely believe they are to blame for the problems themselves. Ironically, people who over-react need people who under-react to complete the interdependence of relationship. Satan who is miserable seeks the misery of all mankind. He tries to spoil our happiness in many ways as he influences us to be out of balance. [47]

We all have the tendency to get out of balance. To have charity is to pray for "Christ-like balances of warmth and strength, mercy and justice, faith and works, love and logic, spontaneity and dignity, [or] flexibility and firmness." [48] To be temperate is to not confuse charity with excessive sympathy. When you have true charity and are temperate you will not only be loving, kind, friendly, soft, gentle, approachable, merciful, and full of love, but you will also be strong, firm, just, consistent, and courageous. True charity reflects a proper balance, of both strength and tenderness. Jesus was full of love and compassion, but he was also firm, just, and strong. And like Him, having a charitable feeling of mercy will not rob a person's sense of justice.

We Are to Be: We Are Not to Be:
Merciful   *Judgmental and unforgiving*

One way of showing mercy is assuming that others are probably doing the best they can according to what they understand. Showing mercy is also to continue to pray for others who hurt or offend us so that both parties can eventually see things from God's point of view. Mercy is to pray that you will be able to extend love, blessings, goodness and prayers to your family members or even enemies. With mercy, the correct question is not "Am I my brother's keeper?" but instead, "Am I my brother's brother?" [49]

There is a reason our Heavenly Father places us with those we associate with here on earth. Elder Maxwell acknowledges the Lord's hand in what he refers to as intersections. "Our friendships are not friendships of initiation at all but are instead friendships of resumption. Each of us has circles of friendships and within those lie the portion of the human family whom God has given us to love to serve and to learn from." [50] Within that circle of associates is provided a laboratory for mercy.

The greatest individual we can learn mercy from is the Lord Jesus Christ. It was Christ's character with His unique combination of celestial attributes which brought him to and got him through Gethsemane and Calvary. He mercifully took into account the varied capacity of others. You and I by contrast sometimes devastate the tender and leave the arrogant unfazed. Part of being merciful is to take into account the capacity of others. Explaining this idea, Brigham Young University Professor Brent Barlow once related the following:

> As a youth in England, Samuel Plimsoll was fascinated with watching ships load and unload their cargoes. He soon observed that, regardless of the cargo space available, each ship had its maximum capacity. If a ship exceeded its limit, it would likely sink at sea. In 1868, Plimsoll entered Parliament and passed a merchant shipping act that, among other things, called for making calculations of how much a ship could carry. As a result, lines were drawn on the hull of each ship in England. As the cargo was loaded, the freighter would sink lower and lower into the water. When the water level on the side of the ship reached the Plimsoll mark, the ship was considered loaded to capacity, regardless of how much space remained. As a result, British deaths at sea were greatly reduced.

> Like ships people have differing capacities at different times and even different days in their lives. In relationships we need to establish our own Plimsoll marks and help identify them in the lives of those we love. Together we need to monitor the load levels and be helpful in shedding or at least adjusting some cargo if we see our sweetheart is sinking. Then, when the ship of love is stabilized, we can evaluate long-term what

has to continue, what can be put off until another time, and what can be put off permanently. Friends, sweethearts, and spouses need to be able to monitor each other's stress and recognize the different tides and seasons of life. We owe it to each other to declare some limits and then help jettison some things if emotional health and strength of loving relationships are at risk. Remember, pure love [or charity] "beareth all things, believeth all things, hopeth all things, and endureth all things," and helps loved ones do the same. [51]

Those who are merciful are aware of the bearing capacities of others. Blessed are the merciful for they will restore and protect others.

We Are to Be:	We Are Not to Be:
Gracious	*Tactless, easily irritated, ungenerous*

When Jesus visited his hometown of Nazareth, the people wondered at his gracious words (Luke 4:22). Being gracious is akin to having charity. Graciousness is to have tact, exhibit control, and be generous in our compliments. A real sense of belonging does matter to each individual in mortality. One of the great things you and I can do for family and friends is to contribute regularly to their storehouses of self-esteem by giving deserved and specific commendations and encouragement. Another thing we can do when we see chaff in the lives of friends as compared with the worthy kernel of their characters is with the breath of graciousness blow the chaff away. [52] Graciousness tells us that all is not fair in love and war. It is something more subtle, something deeper. Graciousness is a love that does not alter with our moods or with external circumstances. Being gracious is exhibited as the idea that "we can have a bad day but still have a good life." [53]

We Are to Be:	**We Are Not to Be:**
Holy	*Worldly*

Eventually the characteristic of holiness will be ours as we receive the gift of charity. As we strip ourselves of fears, jealousies, and doubts we will put off the natural man. The verb strip suggests a painful peeling off of fleshy tendencies rather than gradual erosion. [54] C. S. Lewis in his popular series *The Chronicles of Narnia,* gives us a symbolic narrative of what it is like for our Heavenly Father to strip off the world to make us holy. In Lewis' *The Voyage of the Dawn Treader,* a young boy by the name of Eustace comes upon a dragon's cave. Though he hates dragons, when Eustace is enticed by a treasure inside the cave, he chooses to stay. As Eustace becomes engulfed in the dragon's lair, he does not recognize he has become that which he despised until he realizes that he is running on all fours and sees his own reflection as a dragon in a pool of water. Lewis explains, "He had turned into a dragon while he was asleep. Sleeping on a dragon's hoard with greedy dragonish thoughts in his heart, he had become a dragon himself."

During the subsequent days Eustace tries to "un-dragon" himself by shedding layers of skin like a snake. In explaining his experiences to a friend he confides that to become "un-dragoned" could not be done by yourself, it could be done only by Aslan. In Lewis' chronicles, Aslan is a lion who symbolically represents the Lion of God, or our Savior. Though Eustace was very afraid of feeling the lion's claws, all he wanted was to become a little boy again. Being desperate, Eustace consents to lay flat on his back and let the lion claw at him. Eustace describes, "The very first tear he made was so deep that I thought it had gone right into my heart. And when he began pulling the skin off, it hurt worse than anything I've ever felt. The only thing that made me able to bear it was just the pleasure of feeling the stuff peel off. You know—if you've ever picked the scab of a sore place. It hurts like billy—oh but it is such fun to see it coming away. . . . He peeled the beastly stuff right off. . . . I'd turned into a boy again." [55]

As symbolically described in this story, becoming holy requires a peeling away of those things which we for ourselves cannot remove. As we turn our eternal futures over to the Savior and through repentance are stripped of the world our sense of self worth increases dramatically. "Heavenly Father is in it for the long haul and for all the right reasons and with all the right motivations." [56] He is also in it with the right methodology. When we understand the gift of charity, we will comprehend that it is the most reasonable method of dealing with the human family, including dealing with our own families. What is a person who possesses charity and becomes holy look like? The Apostle Parley P. Pratt describes what it is like to meet one who is holy as follows:

> Their very atmosphere diffuses a thrill, a warm glow of pure gladness and sympathy, to the heart and nerves of others who have kindred feelings, or sympathy of spirit. No matter if the parties are strangers, entirely unknown to each other in person or character; no matter if they have never spoken to each other, each will be apt to remark in his own mind, and perhaps exclaim, when referring to the interview, "O what an atmosphere encircles that stranger! How my heart thrilled with pure and holy feelings in his presence! What confidence and sympathy he inspired! His countenance and spirit gave me more assurance than a thousand written recommendations or introductory letters. [57]

Charity Is the Only Way

Recently a friend of mine came in contact with a woman we will call Stephanie who was everything charity is not. She was the antithesis of the description Parley P. Pratt gives above. My friend found Stephanie to be completely self-absorbed. When others spoke, Stephanie had a glazed look on her face; she was completely uninterested. When Stephanie spoke of herself, she often said things because she thought they would impress others. This woman threw temper tantrums (literally crying) over small, miniscule disruptions, or tiny difficulties. During the course of interaction, Stephanie told my friend of giving a fellow Relief Society sister a ride to an activity and then telling her to find another ride home because in her words, "Charity only goes one way." The amazing thing to my friend was that as she watched Stephanie, who lacked charity, and observed her lack of concern for others, Stephanie's despicable behavior did not seem to matter to some of my friend's associates because this woman was physically attractive. My friend was surprised to find some priesthood bearers she had the greatest respect for "taken in" by Stephanie. They were not attracted to her by anything she did, but only sought Stephanie's company because she was physically beautiful. These associates seemed to be more than willing to overlook immature behavior in this woman.

My friend was amazed as this situation developed before her eyes and found it disheartening. She was so disenchanted that she prayed about it, and the Lord graciously gave an answer to her prayers. While in the temple one day, my friend was thinking about this situation, when the Spirit whispered, "Yes, Stephanie will get a lot of attention here, but remember I the Lord look on the heart. There are those on this earth who also look on the heart. She has so much to change before she can ever be with me."

What Stephanie has failed to learn is that true charity not only goes both ways, it is also the only way. It truly never fails. It is there through thick and thin. It endures through sunshine and shadow, through darkest sorrow and on into the light, it never fails. As Moroni tells us it is "the fountain of all righteousness" (Ether 12:28). Not only does it go both ways, it is the only way to become like Him and to receive an eternal self-esteem.

1. Spencer W. Kimball, "The Abundant Life," *Ensign*, July 1978, 3.

2. Brigham Young, *Journal of Discourses*, 26 vol. (London: Latter-day Saints Book Depot, 1854–86), 7:133–34.

3. Jeffrey R. Holland, "How Do I Love Thee?" *Brigham Young University 1999–2000 Speeches* (Provo: Brigham Young University Press, 2000), 159.

4. Joseph Smith, *Teachings of Prophet Joseph Smith*, comp. Joseph Fielding Smith (Salt Lake City: Deseret Book, 1976), 216.

5. Taylor Hartman, *The Color Code: A New Way to See Yourself, Your Relationships, and Life* (Trabucco Canyon: A Taylor Don Hartman Publication, 1987).

6. Neal A. Maxwell, *Men and Women of Christ* (Salt Lake City: Bookcraft, 1991), 58–59.

7. Richard L. Bednar and Scott R. Peterson, *Spirituality and Self-Esteem: Developing the Inner Self* (Salt Lake City: Deseret Book, 1990), 58.

8. Neal A. Maxwell, "Meekness—A Dimension of True Discipleship," *Ensign*, March 1983, 70.

9. Ester Rasband, *Confronting the Myth of Self-Esteem: Twelve Keys to Finding Peace* (Salt Lake City, Deseret Book, 1998) 123.

10. C. S. Lewis, *Mere Christianity* (New York: Simon & Schuster, 1980) 113–14.

11. Neal A. Maxwell, *Not Withstanding My Weakness* (Salt Lake City: Deseret Book, 1981), 75.

12. Ester Rasband, *Confronting the Myth of Self-Esteem: Twelve Keys to Finding Peace: Twelve Keys to Finding Peace* (Salt Lake City, Deseret Book, 1998), 19.

13. C. S. Lewis, *Mere Christianity* (New York: Touchstone, 1996), 112.

14. Neal A. Maxwell, "The Stern but Sweet Seventh Commandment," *New Era*, June 1979, 36.

15. Spencer W. Kimball, *The Teachings of Spencer W. Kimball*, ed. Edward L. Kimball (Salt Lake City: Bookcraft, 1982), 233.

16. Jeffrey R. Holland, "How Do I Love Thee?" *Brigham Young University 1999–2000 Speeches* (Provo: Brigham Young University Press, 2000), 159.

17. Ester Rasband, *Confronting the Myth of Self-Esteem: Twelve Keys to Finding Peace: Twelve Keys to Finding Peace* (Salt Lake City, Deseret Book, 1998), 49.

18. Joseph F. Smith, *Gospel Doctrine* (Salt Lake City: Deseret Book, 1946), 297–298.

19. Neal A. Maxwell, "Patience," *Ensign*, October 1980, 28.

20. Neal A. Maxwell, "Called to Serve," *Brigham Young University 1993-1994 Devotional and Fireside Speeches*, (Provo: Brigham Young University Press, 1994), 137.

21. Dean Larsen, "The Peaceable Things of The Kingdom," *New Era*, February 1986, 7.

22. Neal A. Maxwell, *Men and Women of Christ* (Salt Lake City: Bookcraft, 1991), 58.

23. Neal A. Maxwell, *Lord, Increase Our Faith* (Salt Lake City: Bookcraft, 1994), 36.

24. Neal A. Maxwell, "The Stern but Sweet Seventh Commandment," *New Era*, June 1979, 36.

25. William Law, *A Serious Call to a Devout and Holy Life* (New York: Paulist Press, 1978), 109.

26. John Taylor, *Journal of Discourses*, 26 vol. (London: Latter-day Saints Book Depot, 1854–86), vol. 12, 81.

27. Jeffrey R. Holland, "How Do I Love Thee?" *Brigham Young University 1999–2000 Speeches* (Provo: Brigham Young University Press, 2000), 159.

28. Neal A. Maxwell, *Lord, Increase Our Faith* (Salt Lake City: Deseret Book, 1994), 115.

29. Jeffrey R. Holland, "How Do I Love Thee?" *Brigham Young University 1999-2000 Speeches* (Provo: Brigham Young University Press, 2000), 159.

30. Ibid., 160.

31. Ibid.

32. William Wordsworth, "Lines written a few miles above Tintern Abbey, on revisiting the banks of the Wye during a tour, July 13, 1798," *Lyrical Ballads 1798* (Oxford: Woodstock Books, 1990), 203.

33. Neal A. Maxwell, "Becometh as a Child," *Ensign*, May 1996, 69.

34. Neal A. Maxwell, *Lord, Increase Our Faith* (Salt Lake City: Bookcraft, 1994), 107.

35. Brigham Young, *Journal of Discourses*, 26 vol. (London: Latter-day Saints Book Depot, 1854–86), 6:74.

36. Neal A. Maxwell, *Lord, Increase Our Faith* (Salt Lake City: Bookcraft, 1994), 108.

37. David O. McKay, "There are Two Roads," *The Improvement Era* 67, February 1964, 84–85.

38. David O. McKay, *The Teachings of David O. McKay*, comp. Mary Jane Woodger, (Salt Lake City: Deseret Book, 2004), 83.

39. Joseph Smith, *Teachings of the Prophet Joseph Smith* (Salt Lake City: Deseret Book, 1976), 220.

40. Neal A. Maxwell, *Lord, Increase Our Faith* (Salt Lake City: Deseret Book, 1994), 25

41. Jeffrey R. Holland, "How Do I Love Thee?" *Brigham Young University 1999–2000 Speeches* (Provo: Brigham Young University Press, 2000), 161.

42. Neal A. Maxwell, "Swallowed Up in the Will of the Father," *Ensign*, November 1995, 24.

43. Stanley Weintraub, *Long Day's Journey into War* (New York: Truman Talley Books/Plume, 1992), 214 and 253.

44. Bryant S. Hinckley, *A Study of the Character and Teachings of Jesus of Nazareth: A Course of Study for the Adult Members of the Aaronic Priesthood* (Salt Lake City: The Church of Jesus Christ of Latter-day Saints, 1950), 169–170, and Dean L. Larsen, "The Peaceable Things of the Kingdom" in *Hope* (Salt Lake City: Deseret Book, 1988), 197–198.

45. Garth L. Allred, *Unlocking the Powers of Faith* (American Fork: Covenant Communications, 1993), 121.

46. Ibid., 113.

47. Ibid., 114–15.

48. Ibid., 143.

49. Neal A. Maxwell, *Wherefore, Ye Must Press Forward* (Salt Lake City: Deseret Book, 1977), 87–88.

50. Neal A. Maxwell, "Brim with Joy (Alma 26:11)," *Brigham Young University 1995–96 Speeches* (1996), 141.

51. Jeffrey R. Holland, "How Do I Love Thee?" *Brigham Young University 1999-2000 Speeches* (Provo: Brigham Young University Press, 2000), 161–162.

52. Neal A. Maxwell, *Deposition of a Disciple* (Salt Lake City: Deseret Book, 1976), 36.

53. Neal A. Maxwell, *Notwithstanding My Weakness* (Salt Lake City: Deseret Book, 1981), 57.

54. C. S. Lewis, *The Chronicles of Narnia* (New York: Harpers Collins Publishers, 2004), 463–66.

55. Ibid., 474–75.

56. Neal A. Maxwell, *Lord, Increase Our Faith* (Salt Lake City: Deseret Book, 1994), 33.

57. Parley P. Pratt, *Key to the Science of Theology* (Salt Lake City: Deseret Book, 1978), 102–103.

Chapter 8
Everybody Has *One*

FAITH, HOPE, AND CHARITY ARE UNIVERSAL. Every soul bound for eternal glory must possess them, and to leave mortality without these three gifts would be disastrous to our eternal progress. However, there are other spiritual gifts that are not universal. These other gifts are individualized and personalized. Some have many gifts and some have few, but all Latter-day Saints have at least one of these individualized, personalized spiritual gifts (D&C 46:11). When we rediscover our individual gifts, we are introduced to a heightened self-worth, and we begin to understand more of whom we were before the veil was drawn.

Elder Neal A. Maxwell explains that these personalized spiritual gifts came with us:

> Each mortal is "endowed" genetically, environmentally, but also premortally. We each have, for instance, at least one spiritual gift. None of the approximately twenty gifts specified in the scriptures is insignificant. Yet, if we despair, then whatever our gifts or talents, we have failed. A gift is no gift until one gives it. Lucifer apparently was and is multi-talented, but his memories of what might have been gnaw at him constantly. No wonder he is an incurable insomniac.[1]

We do not get our individualized spiritual gifts for the first time in mortality. Before the womb, we possessed them. Elder Robert C. Oaks adds,

We are each individuals with talents, strengths, opportunities, and challenges. We're as individual as are our fingerprints or our DNA. Unfortunately, we cannot discover our individuality by just rolling our finger on an ink pad, and then on a clean sheet of paper, or by spitting on a glass laboratory slide as we can with our fingerprints and our DNA. . . . Our particular set of gifts, attitudes, and talents, if properly developed and employed will enable us to fulfill our foreordained purpose. . . . The Lord will lead us in a particular role if we will seek and follow his guidance. [2]

As we redevelop spiritual gifts in mortality, they enhance our experience through this veil of forgetfulness. Especially when we experience fear rather than faith, doubt rather than hope, or jealousy rather than charity, these individualized spiritual gifts act as a buffer against the adversary's attack on our self-respect. "It is important to acknowledge that everyone has gifts and talents." [3] If we deny we possess at least one spiritual gift, we are diminishing our self-worth. Elder Bruce McConkie of the Quorum of the Twelve Apostles promised, "Every converted member of the Church has one or more gifts of the Spirit. . . . If the saints are to be saved, they must accept, understand, and experience the gifts of the Spirit." [4] The spiritual gifts are not optional for the Church of Christ, their existence is mandatory. Moroni promises that gifts come unto every man severally (Moroni 10:17). These gifts are as vital to our modern-day Church as they were during Moroni's time. Moroni places so much emphasis on spiritual gifts that he closes the Book of Mormon by talking about them. Why does he use this subject as the theme of his last and final sermon to those who will live in the fulness of the dispensation of times? Moroni had gone through a full-blown apostasy. For Moroni, one of the alert signs that the apostasy of the church of his dispensation was on its way was the disappearance of spiritual gifts. Trying to prevent our personal apostasy in the latter days, Moroni warns us that spiritual gifts must be part and parcel of any church bearing the name of Jesus Christ. Moroni also warns us that if the day comes that we are not experiencing spiritual gifts in our personal lives, to beware, because "if that day cometh that the power and gifts of God shall be done away among you, it shall be because of unbelief" (Moroni 10:24). Elder Ashton reiterates,

One of the great tragedies of life, it seems to me, is when a person classifies himself as someone who has no talents or gifts. When, in disgust or discouragement, we allow ourselves to reach depressive levels of despair because of our demeaning self-appraisal, it is a sad day for us and a sad day in the eyes of God. For us to conclude that we have no gifts when we judge ourselves by stature, intelligence, grade-point average, wealth, power, position, or external appearance is not only unfair but unreasonable.[5]

Ironically, there are Latter-day Saints who are believers and yet fail to believe they possess any gifts.

Furthermore, Elder McConkie taught that the purpose of spiritual gifts "is to enlighten, encourage, and edify the faithful so that they will inherit peace in this life."[6] Is there anyone who does not desire more security and peace? Peace and security come when we accept our spiritual gifts, understand that we have them, and then experience them to bless others' lives. Many of us are aware of the spiritual gifts of others and yet do not experience our own individualized gifts. One reason for this paradox might be because some Latter-day Saints feel fragmented gift-wise. Not knowing what our gifts are, we may try to be Jacks or Jills of all gifts and masters of none. Such an approach results in feeling fragmented. If we want to have a life of great self-worth, an eternal personality, and a celestial self-image, then we must work on redeveloping specific spiritual gifts rather than trying to develop them all.

A great mortal existence includes a capacity for recognizing and developing individualized gifts. Elder McConkie concurs, "Suffice it to say that true greatness, from an eternal standpoint, is measured not in worldly station nor in ecclesiastical office, but in the possession of the gifts of the Spirit."[7] President Boyd K. Packer has said, "A spiritual gift is an endowment of spiritual power. . . . Spiritual gifts, I repeat, are a product of our faith, and if we do not have them, something is less than it should be."[8]

To be all that we can be, special gifts must be ours. As members of The Church of Jesus Christ of Latter-day Saints, the very first commandment we are given is to receive the Holy Ghost. The Holy Ghost inaugurates the transmission of spiritual gifts to the faithful to assist them through mortality and in remaining true to their baptismal covenants. Elder Robert D. Hales of the Quorum of the Twelve Apostles informs,

> These gifts of the Spirit are encompassed by the gift of the Holy Ghost. The Holy Ghost is the third member of the eternal Godhead and is identified as the Holy Spirit. This Holy Spirit is a gift from God to help us make the decisions that will allow us to find and fulfill our mission. [9]

Given the wonderful blessing of the Holy Ghost, this member of the Godhead brings to worthy Latter-day Saints spiritual gifts that enable them to meet their destinies. Ultimately the "supernal, consummate spiritual gift," the one that is "so simple, and so present that we often ignore it," is that of the Holy Ghost. The Holy Ghost can inspire those who are not members of The Church of Jesus Christ of Latter-day Saints. In fact, his witness is necessary for conversion, but there is a great difference when at baptism we are freely given the presence of this member of the Godhead. [10] As we freely converse with this member of the Godhead, He can bestow His wealth of spiritual gifts.

However, we must always remember that the word "gift" is important. President Boyd K. Packer in speaking of spiritual gifts reminds us,

> I must emphasize that the word gift is of great significance, for a gift may not be demanded or it ceases to be a gift. It many only be accepted when proffered. . . . Spiritual gifts cannot be forced, . . . nor bought, nor earned in the sense that we make some gesture of payment and expect them to automatically be delivered on our own terms.

President Packer then goes on to give us a warning that will be important to remember as we seek to rediscover our own gifts. "There are those who seek such gifts with such persistence that each act moves them farther from them. And in that persistence and determination they place themselves in spiritual danger. Rather, we are to live to be worthy of the gifts, and they will come according to the will of the Lord." [11]

When the Church of Jesus Christ is established and the gift of the Holy Ghost is bestowed, there will be a people who seek after, obtain, and bask in the light of the gifts and wonders of God. Indeed, to deny the gifts of God is to shun or ignore the endowment of the Spirit and to walk in darkness, despair, depression, and doubt—the horrible Ds. We are to come unto Christ, be cleansed by his blood, be filled with his Spirit, and walk in the light of the gifts of that Spirit until we receive the greatest of all the gifts of God: Eternal Life. As we rediscover and redevelop our gifts, we walk in more and more light. Our duty then is to rediscover in mortality what our gifts are, and in turn help others to learn about theirs. Socrates said, "The life which is unexamined is not worth living." [12] Examining our lives as those born of the Spirit includes examining and finding our talents. Elder Ashton taught, "It is up to each of us to search for and build upon the gifts which God has given. We must remember that each of us is made in the image of God, that there are no unimportant persons." [13] In the following chapter, we will discuss ways in which we can rediscover and redevelop our individual spiritual gifts.

1. Neal A. Maxwell, *Deposition of a Disciple* (Salt Lake City: Deseret Book, 1976), 36.

2. Robert C. Oaks, "Understand Who You Are." Brigham Young University Devotional, 21 March 2006, 2.

3. Ibid., 3.

4. Bruce R. McConkie, *Doctrinal New Testament Commentary*, 3 vols. (Salt Lake City: Bookcraft, 1965–1973), 2:366 and 372.

5. Marvin J. Ashton, "There Are Many Gifts," *Ensign*, November 1987, 20.

6. Bruce R. McConkie, *Mormon Doctrine*, 2d ed. (Salt Lake City: Bookcraft, 1966), 314.

7. Bruce R. McConkie, *The Promised Messiah: The First Coming of Christ* (Salt Lake City: Deseret Book, 1978), 574–75.

8. Boyd K. Packer, *The Shield of Faith* (Salt Lake City: Bookcraft, 1998), 101 and 104.

9. Robert D. Hales, "Gifts of the Spirit," *Ensign*, February 2002, 12.

10. Boyd K. Packer, *The Shield of Faith* (Salt Lake City: Bookcraft, 1998), 108.

11. Ibid., 98.

12. Plato, *Euthyphro, Apology, Crito, and Phaedo* (Buffalo, New York: Prometheus Books, 1988), 28. Socrates (470-399 B.C.) spoke these words to the jury in the court of Athens in the year 399 BCE (before the Common Era) after he had been found guilty of heresy and sedition.

13. Marvin J. Ashton, "There Are Many Gifts," *Ensign*, November 1987, 20.

Chapter 9
Rediscovering Our Individual Gifts

SPIRITUAL GIFTS BELONG TO THE CHURCH OF JESUS CHRIST. As the spiritual gifts are exercised in the lives of Latter-day Saints, they provide evidence that The Church of Jesus Christ of Latter-day Saints is true. The scriptures are replete with the assignment to members of Christ's true Church to seek after spiritual gifts. Paul instructed the Corinthians, "Now concerning spiritual gifts . . . I would not have you ignorant. . . . but covet earnestly the best gifts" (1 Corinthians 12:1 and 31). Moroni instructs that we should "come unto Christ, and lay hold upon every good gift" (Moroni 10:30). At the same time, the scriptures are also replete with a warning that we are not to seek after signs. Jesus Christ in his own ministry declared, "An evil and adulterous generation seeketh after a sign" (Matthew 12:39 and Luke 11:29). This declaration is repeated in the Doctrine and Covenants,

> And he that seeketh signs shall see signs, but not unto salvation.
>
> Verily, I say unto you, there are those among you who seek signs, and there have been such even from the beginning;
>
> But, behold, faith cometh not by signs, but signs follow those that believe.
>
> Yea, signs come by faith, not by the will of men, nor as they please, but by the will of God. (63:7–10).

So on the one hand, Saints are encouraged to seek the best gifts (D&C 46:8) and yet the Lord also warns that he is not pleased with those who seek "after signs and wonders for faith" (D&C 63:12). Clarification between these two commandments is needed.

President Packer looks at these two directives as counterbalancing one another and defines the difference between seeking spiritual gifts and signs as follows: "A spiritual gift is an endowment of power. . . . Signs, on the other hand, are evidences of visible manifestations that a spiritual power is present. . . . Spiritual gifts and the signs that follow them are the product of faith and not the reverse—faith is not an outgrowth of the signs." [1]

We Are Commanded to Ask for Spiritual Gifts

As we increase our faith, we will receive spiritual gifts from the Holy Ghost. However, unlike receiving a Christmas or birthday present, spiritual gifts will not mysteriously appear at the right time from someone who loves us. Spiritual gifts do not come automatically or easily. Instead, we must ask for the spiritual gifts and "ardently desire [them] in a righteous way." [2] Scholar Hugh Nibley admonished,

> We can't conjure them [spiritual gifts] up for ourselves. The Lord gives them, and he says he gives them. We must ask for them with real intent and with an honest heart. We can have them—any gift. And a nice protective clause is written in there: If we're not supposed to have a gift, what we *are* worthy of, what *is* beneficial or expedient, we shall have *that*. . . . All these things are available—all we need to do is ask. But we must *ask* for them, and of course if we ask not we receive not. The gifts are not in evidence today, except one gift, which you notice the people *ask* for—the gift of healing. They ask for that with honest intent and with sincere hearts, and we really do have that gift. Because we are desperate and nobody else can help us, we ask with sincere hearts of our Lord. As for these other gifts, how often do we ask for them? How earnestly do we seek for them? We could have them if we did

ask, but we don't. "Well, who denies them?" Anyone who doesn't ask for them. They are available to all for the asking, but one must ask with an honest heart, sincerely.[3]

If all the spiritual gifts are available to us, as Nibley suggests above, our problem is not asking for gifts but rather in deciding what gift to ask for. In not deciding which gift is needed and failing to ask for specific gifts of the Spirit, many of us live far below our privileges. President Brigham Young said, "If a person lives according to the revelations given to God's people, he may have the Spirit of the Lord to signify to him his will, and to guide and direct him in the discharge of his duties, in his temporal as well as his spiritual exercises. I am satisfied, however, that in this respect, we live far beneath our privileges."[4] According to President Young, we can have the opportunity more often than we do to have the Lord help us in our daily lives. As we get on our knees, we can ask specific questions such as, "Lord what do I need to do? What will I be good at? What gift will make a difference in my life?" It will then be our right to receive instruction from our Heavenly Father. President George Q. Cannon of the First Presidency gives other questions we might ask below:

> How many of you . . . are seeking for these gifts that God has promised to bestow? How many of you, when you bow before your Heavenly Father in your family circle or in your secret places, contend for these gifts to be bestowed upon you? How many of you ask the Father in the name of Jesus, to manifest Himself to you through these powers and these gifts? Or do you go along day by day like a door turning on its hinges, without having any feeling upon the subject, without exercising any faith whatever; content to be baptized and be members of the Church, and to rest there, thinking that your salvation is secure because you have done this?
>
> If any of us are imperfect, it is our duty to pray for the gift that will make us perfect. Have I imperfections? I am full of them. What is my duty? To pray to God to give me the gifts that will correct these imperfections.

If I am an angry man, it is my duty to pray for charity, which suffereth long and is kind. Am I an envious man? It is my duty to seek for charity, which
envieth not. So with all the gifts of the Gospel. They
are intended for this purpose. No man ought to say
. . . that God has promised to give strength to correct
these things, and to give gifts that will eradicate them.
If a man lack wisdom, it is his duty to ask God for
wisdom. The same with everything else. That is the
design of God concerning His Church. He wants His
Saints to be perfected in truth. For this purpose He
gives these gifts, and bestows them upon those who
seek after them, in order that they may be a perfect
people upon the face of the earth, notwithstanding
their many weaknesses, because God has promised to
give the gifts that are necessary for their perfection. [5]

As Paul commanded, we are to "covet earnestly the best gifts"
(1 Corinthians 12:31). In prayer, we can ask for specific gifts when
needed, and then we will feel the wonderful joy of being an instru-
ment in the Lord's hands. The following story is told about President
Heber J. Grant, who asked in prayer for a specific gift and received it at
the very moment it was needed. "While Elder Grant was serving in the
Quorum of the Twelve Apostles, his testimony of the Prophet Joseph
contributed to the conversion of his half brother Fred, "who had been
careless, indifferent, and wayward, and who had evinced no interest in
the gospel of Jesus Christ." [6]

Elder Grant was in the Salt Lake Tabernacle one day,
preparing to give a talk, when he saw Fred enter the
building. He recounted:

"When . . . I saw Fred for the first time in the Tabernacle, and realized that he was seeking God
for light and knowledge regarding the divinity
of this work, I bowed my head and I prayed that
if I were requested to address the audi-ence, the Lord
would inspire me by the revelation of His Spirit, to
speak in such manner that my brother would have
to acknowledge to me that I had spoken beyond my
natural ability, that I had been inspired of the Lord. I

realized that if he made that confession, then I should be able to point out to him that God had given him a testimony of the divinity of this work."

When it was his turn to speak, Elder Grant walked to the pulpit and opened a book to guide him in the address he had prepared to give. He then said to the congregation, "I cannot tell you just why, but never before in all my life have I desired so much the inspiration of the Lord as I desire it today." He "asked the people for their faith and prayers" and continued with his own silent petition for inspiration. After speaking for 30 minutes, he returned to his seat. He later recalled:

"When I sat down after my talk, I remembered that my book was still lying open on the pulpit. President George Q. Cannon [First Counselor in the First Presidency] was sitting just behind me . . . , and I heard him say to himself: 'Thank God for the power of that testimony!' When I heard this, I remembered that I had forgotten the sermon I had intended to deliver, and the tears gushed from my eyes like rain, and I rested my elbows on my knees and put my hands over my face, so that the people by me could not see that I was weeping like a child. I knew when I heard those words of George Q. Cannon that God had heard and answered my prayer. I knew that my brother's heart was touched.

"I [had] devoted my thirty minutes almost entirely to a testimony of my knowledge that God lives, that Jesus is the Christ, and to the wonderful and marvelous labors of the Prophet Joseph Smith, bearing witness to the knowledge God had given me that Joseph Smith was in very deed a prophet of the true and living God.

"The next morning, my brother came into my office and said, 'Heber, I was at a meeting yesterday and heard you preach.'

"I said, 'The first time you ever heard your brother preach, I guess?'

" 'Oh, no,' he said, 'I have heard you many times. I generally come in late and go into the gallery. I often go out before the meeting is over. But you never spoke as you did yesterday. You spoke beyond your natural ability. You were inspired of the Lord.' These were the identical words I had uttered the day before, in my prayer to the Lord!

"I said to him, 'Are you still praying for a testimony of the gospel?'

"He said, 'Yes, and I am going nearly wild.'

"I asked, 'What did I preach about yesterday?'

"He replied, 'You know what you preached about.'

"I said, 'Well, you tell me.'

" 'You preached upon the divine mission of the Prophet Joseph Smith.'

"I answered, 'And I was inspired beyond my natural ability; you have never heard me speak at any time as I spoke yesterday. Do you expect the Lord to get a club and knock you down? What more testimony do you want of the gospel of Jesus Christ than that a man speaks beyond his natural ability and under the inspiration of God, when he testifies of the divine mission of the Prophet Joseph Smith.'

"The next Sabbath he applied to me for baptism." [7]

In the story related above, President Grant requested a specific gift and then received it. He was very aware of the Lord's ability to bestow a spiritual gift at a given time when it was most needed.

At the same time, we need not worry about asking for gifts we are unprepared to exercise. The Prophet Joseph Smith promised,

"Now concerning spiritual gifts, I would not have you ignorant". . . . You will receive instructions through the order of the Priesthood which God has established, through the medium of those appointed to lead, guide and direct the affairs of the Church in this last dispensation. . . . The Saints whose integrity has been tried and proved faithful, might know how to ask the Lord and receive an answer. . . . If you do right, there is no danger of your going too fast. . . . [God does] not care how fast we run the path of virtue.[8]

As promised, the Lord will not let us have more gifts than we can handle. He is not like an overindulgent parent on Christmas morning. However, sometimes we are like a little child who is so scared that when he or she sits on Santa Claus's knee we forget to ask for anything. Elder Bruce R. McConkie clarified, "We are commanded to seek the gifts of the Spirit; if we do not do so, we are not walking in that course which is pleasing to Him whose gifts they are."[9] Moroni commanded, "Lay hold upon every good gift" (Moroni 10:30). How do you and I get a hold of the spiritual gifts? We begin to lay hold of them simply by asking for them. The important question is not whether or not spiritual gifts are available. Instead the question to ask is what gift do each of us need. The Lord has given some guidelines for knowing what particular gifts each of us can lay hold of. Usually some hints are imbedded in our patriarchal blessings.

Studying Our Patriarchal Blessings Brings Insight to Spiritual Gifts

Much has been said about the purpose of our patriarchal blessings. Church educator Karl G. Maeser spoke of patriarchal blessings as "paragraphs from the book of your possibilities." President Harold B. Lee promised that "If we read our patriarchal blessings, we will see what the spirit of prophecy has held up to us as to what each of us can become."[10] Elder Hartman Rector Jr., emeritus member of the Quorum of the Seventy, calls it "one's spiritual DNA chart."[11] And President Thomas S. Monson promised that "just as the Lord provided a Liahona to Lehi, that same Lord provides for you and for me a rare and priceless gift . . . your patriarchal blessing."[12]

Giving and receiving patriarchal blessings is a unique practice in the Lord's Church. The process involved in giving and receiving a patriarchal blessing is also unique.

As the patriarch seeks the Spirit he may be moved to give admonitions, promises, and assurances. Individual traits of personality and strengths and weaknesses may be mentioned. Against the backdrop of the prophetic anticipation of world events, individual roles and callings may be named. One's spiritual gifts, talents, skills, and potentials may be specified with their associated obligations of gratitude and dedication. [13]

Along these same lines, President Ezra Taft Benson remarked:

I am glad Beethoven found his way into music, Rembrandt into art, Michelangelo into sculpturing, and President David O. McKay into teaching. To find your proper niche and do well at it can bless you, yours, and your fellowmen. If you need help in finding your career, it is available: Ponder and pray about it; study closely your patriarchal blessing; consider what you do well; take some vocational and interest tests; and get acquainted with various professions to see what is available. [14]

In addition, John A. Widtsoe, of the Quorum of the Twelve, speaking of patriarchal blessings has instructed,

Our special needs may be pointed out; special gifts may be promised us; we may be blessed to overcome our weaknesses, to resist temptation, or to develop our powers, so that we may the more surely achieve the promised blessings. Since all men differ, their blessings may differ; but a patriarchal blessing always confers promises upon us, becomes a warning against failure in life, and a means of guidance in attaining the blessings of the Lord. It may be made of daily help in all the affairs of life.

These blessings are possibilities predicated upon faithful devotion to the cause of truth. They must be earned. Otherwise they are but empty words. Indeed, they rise to their highest value when used as ideals, specific possibilities, toward which we may strive throughout life. . . . He helps us by pointing out the divine goal which we may enjoy if we pay the price. [15]

In most cases, our patriarchal blessings can identify spiritual gifts for us. Elder Robert C. Oaks of the First Quorum of Seventy stated,

> One of the purposes of patriarchal blessings is to identify our special gifts and talents. Through these blessings the Lord can help us focus our attention and awareness on particular fields of interests in which we are especially adept. These blessings can serve an important role in helping us to understand who we are in God's plan. We should read them carefully, re-read them, and then endeavor to live our lives in such a way that the Lord can bless us in all of the ways that he has promised us. [16]

However, many times those gifts may be veiled within vague wording, and it is only by studying our blessings that spiritual gifts can be revealed. The Lord never gives the dole. He expects us to work in discovering the meaning of statements made in our patriarchal blessings. For instance, my patriarchal blessing has an interesting sentence. I am told I have some gifts I do not realize I possess, but I am also promised they will be manifested when they will be needed.

Some of us may feel a bit disappointed in the lack of detail found in our patriarchal blessing about our spiritual gifts. I remember in college I was dating a young man and made the mistake of sharing my blessing with him, and he shared his with me. The reading of my blessing was an easy task for him. The reading of his was not. It was long. It was detailed. It was remarkable! It told him what his profession was to be, how he was to prepare himself for that profession, and that in that very profession he would meet his wife. When we were through reading each other's blessings, he turned to me and said, "I am so sorry." He felt bad for me because he felt my blessing was skimpy compared to his. From this experience I learned length is not a factor of importance with patriarchal blessings. Over the years, I have watched him ignore the details of his blessing and some of those promises have not yet unfolded in his life. President James E. Faust tells us that his blessing is very short but wholly adequate for him. [17] Every time I read my own blessing, different statements have focus. At times, through short paragraphs I am taught about a gift I did not know previously existed. Others have experienced this same thing. Below are some examples of those who studied their blessings and subsequently had their gifts manifest.

When President Joseph Fielding Smith was ordained an apostle in 1910, the *Salt Lake Tribune* published criticisms against him, his father, and the Smith family for nepotism.[18] This vilification ignored his qualifications for the apostleship. During this difficult time, he took refuge in the words of his patriarchal blessing. He had been told, "It shall be thy duty to sit in council with thy brethren, and to preside among the people."[19] President Smith had been told that it was his gift to be a Church leader long before the opportunity came along, and at a time of trouble, those words provided comfort.

President Spencer W. Kimball was told in his blessing, "You will preach the gospel to many people, but more especially to the Lamanites, for the Lord will bless you with the gift of the language and power to portray before that people the gospel in great plainness."[20] What do think President Kimball thought when he lost his vocal chords and yet had been promised the gift of the language? Those who listened to this great prophet know the language he was blessed with was not Spanish or Navajo; it was the language of the Spirit.

Sometimes lines in another's patriarchal blessing can provide insight also. For instance, President Marion G. Romney of the First Presidency, was comforted by a line in his wife's blessing. He disclosed:

> I had married the girl of my dreams. . . . She had been the valedictorian of her graduating class at Brigham Young University. She was so much better educated and prepared for the responsibilities of married life than I was that except for her patriarchal blessing I would have been mortified with an inferiority complex. The patriarch . . . spared me this humiliation by telling her, long before I met her, that she "would win and keep the love of a man who was her equal."[21]

I have also found that gifts and promises in patriarchal blessings can be passed down to posterity. One example of this comes from a lesser known personality. Carl W. Beuhner tells us of his father's desire after coming to the Salt Lake Valley. His father wanted to become a cement contractor. Cement at that time was sort of a miracle product that had not been on the market too long, and Carl's father saw in it great possibilities. He began working with cement. Buehner relates:

While this art was still in its very elemental stage, my father received his patriarchal blessing. Among other wonderful things said in this blessing was stated that he and his sons would help erect temples for this Church. At the time this blessing was given, there was no possibility or idea in the world that such a thing could ever happen. . . . I can tell you as of today, we have done considerable work on ten temples. My father has been dead for twenty-five years; and yet, I have seen the fulfillment of his patriarchal blessing all but to the letter. [22]

As was Carl Beuhner's experience, we can fulfill our ancestors blessings, sharing in "family gifts" after they have left mortality. This also happened in my life. My father was told in his patriarchal blessing that his testimony would be heard across the airways. As far as I know, my father never spoke over radio or television. After he passed away, I thought, "Well I guess that part of his blessing will have to happen in the millennium." Then one day while listening to myself relate an incident from my father's life on KBYU, the Spirit whispered to me, "You have just fulfilled your father's patriarchal blessing. You have born your father's testimony across the airways."

Paying Attention to Compliments
Enlightens Our Understanding of Our Gifts

Besides studying our patriarchal blessings to discover our spiritual gifts, we can also pay attention to compliments given to us by others. Paying attention to those compliments may include our noticing what comes easily or naturally. We will want to pay attention to what we enjoy doing, and those activities often bring compliments. We can identify what seems to be second nature to us, because we do have a second nature that came with us through the veil.

As a young nineteen-year-old student teacher, I remember being told by my supervisor, "You are a natural born teacher." I knew what was meant, but now I would disagree. I was not born as a teacher. Rather, gifts do not come at birth; gifts come with us premortally. For me, teaching came easily even when I was a little girl. I remember in the third grade being assigned to give an oral report. I did not think much about it or prepare, I just got up when it was my turn and jabbered for a few minutes. Afterwards, my little classmate said to me in frustration, "That was great! How did you do that? I haven't seen you even prepare." I replied, "I don't know." Early on as I received compliments, I realized that teaching and speaking in front of others came easily.

Compliments we receive and what others notice about us are key in discovering our talents. As we pay attention to compliments, it will be a hint to skills, aptitudes, and abilities the Lord expects us to redevelop. If we do not develop those gifts, they will be taken away from us either in mortality or hereafter. Elder Bruce R. McConkie warns:

> Every man must use such talents as he may have or they will be lost. If a man cannot compose music, perhaps he can sing in the choir, if he cannot write books, at least he can read them; if he cannot paint pictures, he can learn to appreciate the artistry of others; if he cannot achieve preeminence in one specific field, so be it, he can still succeed in his own field; for each man has some talent, and he will be judged on the basis of how he uses what he has.

> It is an eternal law of life that we either progress or retrogress; they will increase their talents and abilities, or those they have wither and die. No one stands still; there is no such thing as pure neutrality. [23]

Sometimes the Lord will even give us talents and gifts in spite of ourselves and our weaknesses in order to bless others. For instance, we may have known someone who can teach with the Spirit but does not always live by the Spirit. However, eventually, if we do not fully develop those talents within the framework of the gospel of Jesus Christ, that which comes easily will be taken away.

Accepting and Fulfilling Callings Develops Gifts

Accepting and magnifying callings can also help us to identify and develop spiritual gifts. I have found that the Lord blesses us with callings through his priesthood leaders where we personally need growth, and we can often serve beyond our natural abilities. As the Lord stretches us, spiritual gifts will manifest themselves in callings as needed. Elder Maxwell promised, "God does not begin by asking about our ability, but only about availability, and if we then prove our dependability, he increases our capability." [24]

There may or may not be a pattern in our callings. There was a definite pattern to my church callings as the Lord prepared me for my present career. Up until obtaining my position at Brigham Young University, I only had two callings in my adult life, and I was called to one of those positions by nine different bishops. Once, I walked into a new ward, and the bishop did not even know my name when he called me to this certain calling. That calling was being a Gospel doctrine teacher. Since starting to teach at Brigham Young University, the Lord has given me different opportunities, but before that, he was preparing me to teach the Gospel professionally. It was interesting to watch my bishops facilitate those opportunities by listening to the Spirit. One gift bishops are promised with the mantle of their calling is the ability to discern the gifts of their ward members. The Lord often inspires our priesthood leaders to provide callings where we can develop our gifts.

Paying Attention to Promptings Gives Us Opportunities to Redevelop Gifts

Peter Marshall, one of the greatest chaplains of the United States Congress, wrote in the last prayer before his death, "Deliver us, our Father . . . where we cannot convince, let us be willing to persuade, for small deeds done are better than great deeds planned." [25] Little things completed can heighten our opportunity to redevelop talents. Along the same line, the Lord may prompt us to seize little opportunities that may become very important episodes throughout our lives in redeveloping spiritual gifts. These opportunities will ultimately bring us self-esteem, because we will come to know that the Lord is directing us and is with us. President Thomas S. Monson has identified these important moments as "small hinges." He instructed, "I have been thinking recently about choices and their consequences. It has been said that the gate of history turns on small hinges, and so do people's lives. The choices we make determine our destiny."[26] The Prophet Joseph Smith further instructed, "We consider that God has created man with a mind capable of instruction, and a faculty which may be enlarged in proportion to the heed and diligence given to the light communicated from heaven to the intellect."[27]

This light communicated from heaven will help us at times to identify our spiritual gifts. We do not redevelop our spiritual gifts in a moment, but there are defining moments where redeveloping our gifts turns on very small experiences, and if we miss one of those moments, it may slow down or impede the redevelopment of a certain gift. These decisions we make as far as our spiritual gifts are concerned are often made by preference rather than principle. Temple-worthy Latter-day Saints for the most part do not struggle with decisions whether or not to keep telestial commandments; rather, their difficult decisions often deal with quandaries such as, "How do I best use my time?" Promptings about these kinds of decisions must be paid attention to. Joseph instructed we will receive "sudden strokes of ideas."[28] Promptings often comes in short, crisp phrases, impressing upon us a certain direction. And with those promptings, the Holy Ghost will testify of the truthfulness of all things, including our spiritual gifts. Elder Maxwell assures us,

> We sometimes think of defining moments. These defining moments in our lives usually focus on single episodes that can sometimes outwardly, as well as inwardly, sometimes be quite dramatic. Yet these defining moments are usually proceeded by small subtle preparatory moments. Moreover the defining moments are also followed by many smaller moments that are shaped by preceding and defining moments. . . .

Be assured that God is "in the details" and in the subtleties of the defining moments and the preparatory moments. He will reassure you. He will remind you. Sometimes, if you're like me, he will sometimes reprove you in a highly personal process not understood or appreciated by those outside the context.[29]

The Holy Ghost is willing to be in the details of our lives, and he will be in the details of helping our eternal identities blossom. If we will but listen, and then seize those opportunities it will open our lives to redeveloping spiritual gifts.

Studying Spiritual Gifts as Described in the Scriptures

When the Lord repeats himself in scripture, He is placing importance on a subject. Three scriptural accounts all testify of the same ideas, and principles describing the spiritual gifts in detail. If we look at the context of these passages, they take even more significance. Section 46 of the Doctrine and Covenants is a warning to early Saints of this dispensation to beware of people with false gifts. In this section the Lord explains how the Holy Ghost works and describes the kinds of gifts the Holy Spirit gives. Second, in the New Testament, Paul is losing ground as he sees the Great Apostasy coming. He tells the Corinthians that when spiritual gifts disappear, you know that you are in a state of apostasy. Third, as we have already mentioned, is Moroni's discourse on the gifts of the spirit. Moroni had experienced full-blown apostasy and chose to end his record by talking about spiritual gifts. Elder Jeffrey R. Holland describes Moroni's predicament:

In this state of lonely witnessing, Moroni was shown the last days of another civilization—our own. And Moroni saw they would be very much like his own. In these days it would be said that miracles were done away, and secret combinations would delight in works of darkness. Fires and tempests and vapors of smoke would singe the earth, while wars, rumors of wars, and earthquakes would rage in divers places. Pollutions would come upon the face of the earth, including the moral pollution of murders, robbery, lying, whoredoms, and "all manner of abominations." Even churches would be defiled, lifted up in the pride of their hearts. They would be built up to get gain and to offer forgiveness of sins through the payment of money, becoming as polluted as the physical and moral environment around them.[30]

Amidst that prologue, Moroni tells us what will save us along with saving our individual self-image amidst such an immoral environment. Those saving devices are the spiritual gifts.

Paul, Moroni, and Joseph Smith list the spiritual gifts in pairs. Spiritual gifts are to be used to serve others, and service is where self-esteem blooms. Paul explains that just as there are different offices and callings in the Church, so the various spiritual gifts are given to different individuals so they can function together as the members of the human body. Every part of the body is necessary for its proper function. No part of the body can claim independence from another. In this same way spiritual gifts are interdependent; therefore, the Lord lists spiritual gifts linked together (Ephesians 4:16). These gift pairs are listed and described below in the sequence they are found in Doctrine and Covenants, section 46.

To Know that Jesus is the Christ & To Believe on His Words

The gift to know that Jesus is the Christ is placed first among the scriptural gifts. To believe that Jesus of Nazareth was the Anointed One, the Messiah, and that He was crucified for the sins of the world, is different than knowing it. Such knowledge is chief among the spiritual gifts. When one hears the words of one who is the possessor of this gift, the hearer also receives a witness of the Holy Ghost that the bearer of the testimony has that knowledge. Brigham Young explained this once while speaking in the tabernacle. When he looked down and saw the missionary who converted him, Eleazar Miller, Brigham Young said that when Eleazar Miller said the Church was true, "I knew he knew the Church was true."[31] "Their testimony was like fire in my bones; I understood the spirit of their teaching."[32] Such is the gift of knowing that Jesus is the Christ.

This wonderful gift of knowing Jesus is the Christ has an associate gift explained as follows:

> To some it is given by the Holy Ghost to know that Jesus Christ is the Son of God, and that he was crucified for the sins of the world.
>
> To others it is given to believe on their words, that they also might have eternal life if they continue faithful. (D&C 46:13–14)

At the age of eighteen, these two verses became very important to me. During the summer after my high school graduation, I was chosen to be a participant in the Hill Cumorah pageant. Fresh out of high school as one of the youngest participants, I felt very intimidated during the first days of travel. After three days on a bus conversing with young men and women who seemed so much more knowledgeable than I, I found myself at a testimony meeting held in South Bend, Indiana. After over two hours of listening to powerful testimonies from other tour participants, I was feeling very inadequate in my testimony when a young returned missionary brought me great reassurance.

As he began his testimony, he quoted the scriptures listed above. He then spoke words that comforted my heart, "If there are any of you who are feeling that your testimony is weak compared to those you have heard today, I would just encourage you to refer often to section 46 verses 13 and 14. Notice if you continue to be faithful and believe in others' words, you also will receive Eternal Life." With those comforting words, I became the recipient of a spiritual gift given freely by another pageant participant, and as promised, I too eventually came to know for myself that Jesus is the Christ.

Those who continue faithfully and believe on others' words will ultimately be blessed to know also. Eventually every knee will bow and every tongue will confess that Jesus is the Christ, but until then, it is a gift to be able to hang on to the testimony of those who have the gift of knowing. President Harold B. Lee explained this associate gift as follows:

> I know, as the Spirit has borne witness to my soul, that the Savior lives. To you who may not have that

testimony, may I ask you to hold to my testimony until you have developed one for yourselves. But work on it, study, and pray until you too can know with a certainty that these things are true—that God lives and this is the plan of salvation.[33]

The Difference of Administrations & The Diversities of Operations

There are a number of explanations regarding this pair of gifts. Some have said that these scriptures refer to the different divisions of the courses of Levite priests or the two divisions of the priesthood, Melchizedek and Aaronic. Others have said that a diversity of operations refers to being able to recognize various spiritual influences. These are viable explanations, and these spiritual gifts can be manifest in many ways. Moroni clarifies, "there are different ways that these gifts are administered; but it is the same God who worketh all in all" (Moroni 10:8).

For me, the differences of administrations and diversities of operations is manifest most clearly in Church leadership. I tell my students to look at their bishopric as an example of these two gifts. There will probably be one member of a bishopric usually, but it is not always the bishop, who is a minister to the ward. This person is very keen to the trials of life, the hardships and tears people are experiencing, and they minister to those whom they serve. On the other hand, there will also be a member of the bishopric who takes care of the operation of the ward. This person is on top of such details as making sure there is a printed program, that there are speakers for Sacrament meeting, and that members are set apart to their various callings. Sometimes those exercising these gifts change back and forth, but both are needed on a constant basis in a bishopric, a Relief Society Presidency, or the First Presidency. To one is given to minister to the emotional and spiritual needs of the congregation, and to another is given to make sure things operate smoothly. In a Relief Society, these gifts might be manifest in the work of the compassionate service committee verses and the Home, Family, and Personal Enrichment activities. Both of these gifts are needed and are interdependent.

The Word of Wisdom &
The Word of Knowledge

The knowledge the Lord speaks of as the word of knowledge in this instance is not random; rather, this knowledge specifically refers to knowledge of the Gospel and the gift of being able to instruct others. There are differences in the gifts of wisdom, knowledge, and the ability to instruct. Knowledge is a carefully stored-up supply of facts, generally slowly acquired. "According to Coleridge, 'common sense in an uncommon degree' is what men call *wisdom*."[34] Wisdom is almost a direct operation of intuition. The ability to instruct is the gift to impart of this supply to others. Wisdom is the ability to apply that knowledge, or the judgment necessary to the application of wisdom, and is more functional. Knowledge is more abstract. President J. Rueben Clark of the First Presidency further explains the difference between the word of wisdom and the word of knowledge:

> Knowledge is the handmaid of wisdom and waits always upon her bidding.
>
> Knowledge plants the seed; wisdom garners the harvest.
>
> Knowledge digs deep for hidden secrets, wisdom tells them openly that they must be put to wise use.
>
> Knowledge sees, feels, and listens; wisdom finds out and gives the lesson.
>
> Knowledge is the race of the swift, the battle of the strong; wisdom is that which endureth to the end.
>
> Knowledge like the wind goeth where it listeth; wisdom braves the blasts and goeth down the middle of the road.
>
> Knowledge worketh in darkness; wisdom laboreth in the full day sun.
>
> Knowledge crieth aloud her excellence; wisdom silently doeth mighty works.
>
> Knowledge telleth the hours of the sun's coming up and going down; wisdom putteth the hours to the service of man.

Knowledge telleth the time for sowing and for reaping; wisdom planneth wisely and nurseth the crop to ripeness.

Knowledge counts the virtues and marks out their boundaries; wisdom brings them all together to make the upright man. [35]

As explained above, the gifts of knowledge and wisdom are also interdependent.

Faith to Be Healed &
The Faith to Heal

The gifts of healing and the faith to be healed are associated with the gift of faith. (Moroni 7:35–37). These two gifts are jointly experienced by the person who needs healing and exhibits faith and the one who is the healer. It is a powerful thing for a priesthood holder to stand in the place of God and exercise priesthood power in order to help those who are sick and afflicted. It is also a powerful thing to have enough faith in Jesus Christ that you can be healed of an illness or affliction. A special divine power is needed by both entities.

The Prophet Joseph Smith is one who displayed the gift of healing. One occasion when he used this spiritual gift was in the case of healing Elsa Johnson's arm. Mrs. Johnson along with her husband and others came to visit the prophet in Kirtland in 1831. During the conversation that ensued, Mrs. Johnson who had been afflicted with a lame arm and was not able to raise it above her head asked if there were anyone on the earth who could heal physical maladies. The Prophet then took Mrs. Johnson by her hand and said, "Woman, in the name of the Lord Jesus Christ, I command thee to be whole." Mrs. Johnson at once lifted up her arm, and the next day was able to do her washing which she had not been able to do for some time. [36] Such healings have continued in The Church of Jesus Christ of Latter-day Saints as members and priesthood holders exhibit faith to be healed and faith to heal.

Prophecy &

The Discerning of Spirits

To prophesy is to speak in the name of the Lord, of things present, past, or future. The discerning of spirits is when those who hear prophecy are blessed to discern the spirit by which such prophecy comes. The discerning of Spirits can also be referred to as being a good judge of character. President Heber C. Kimball of the First Presidency had the gift of prophecy highly developed, and at times it seemed "he could see into the future as if it were an open book,"[37] However, there were those who heard him prophesy who lacked the complementary gift to discern the spirit. Apostle Orson F. Whitney explained the following situation in which Heber C. Kimball displayed the gift of prophecy, and those who heard discerned incorrectly:

> It was during this time of famine, when half starved, half-clad settlers scarcely knew where to look for the next crust of bread or for rags to hide their nakedness . . . that Heber C. Kimball, filled with the spirit of prophecy, in a public meeting declared to the astonished congregation that, within a short time, "States goods" would be sold in the streets of Great Salt Lake City cheaper than in New York and that the people should be abundantly supplied with food and clothing.
>
> "I don't believe a word of it," said Charles C. Rich; and he but voiced the sentiment of nine-tenths of those who had heard the astonishing declaration.
>
> Heber himself was startled at his own words. . . . He remarked to the brethren that he was afraid he "had missed it this time." But they were not his own words, and He who had inspired them knew how to fulfill.
>
> The occasion for the fulfillment of this remarkable prediction was the unexpected advent of the gold-hunters, on their way to California. . . . Salt Lake Valley became the resting place, . . . and before the Saints had had time to recover from their surprise at Heber's temerity in making such a prophecy, the still

more wonderful fulfillment was brought to their very doors. . . . Impatient at their [the miners'] slow progress, in order to lighten their loads, they threw away or "sold for a song" the valuable merchandise with which they had stored their wagons to cross the Plains. . . . Thus, as the Prophet Heber had predicted, "States goods" were actually sold in the streets of Great Salt Lake City cheaper than they could have been purchased in the City of New York.[38]

Another way the gift of prophecy is displayed is when those with this gift share a testimony of Jesus. A person who comes to know concerning the future, to have great views of that which is to come by the power the gift of the Holy Ghost, also comes to know that Jesus is the Lord and Redeemer. The gift of prophecy is but an extension of revelation.[39] This gift is the privilege of every Latter-day Saint and as President Wilford Woodruff promised, it can be experienced daily by the faithful. President Woodruff said that "it is the privilege of every man and woman in this kingdom to enjoy the spirit of prophecy, which is the spirit of God; and to the faithful it reveals such things as are necessary for their comfort and consolation, and to guide them in their daily duties."[40]

Gifts of Tongues &
The Interpretations of Tongues

The Prophet Joseph Smith clarified that some gifts are of more worth and importance than others:

There are only two gifts that could be made visible— the gift of tongues and the gift of prophecy.

The gift of tongues is the *smallest gift* perhaps of the whole, and yet it is one that is the most sought after.

The greatest, the best, and the most useful gifts would be known nothing about by an observer.[41]

The prophet went on to tell Church members that if they were to speak in tongues, it would be only for their own comfort and was "not to be received for doctrine"[42] or to be used to dictate or control the Church, for those manifestations were still under the control of the priesthood. [43] He also warned that the gift of tongues should never be used without interpretation. One reason for this warning was that "the devil can speak in tongues." [44] The gift of tongues is given to men on earth to enable them to preach the Gospel in a more effective manner, as well as to offer and express praise, thanksgiving, and feelings of rapture to the Lord of love in a way that brings peace to the soul. There seems to be at least three manifestations of the gift of tongues.

One manifestation takes place when individuals are enabled to speak with ease or with fluency in a foreign but known language. This gift is often manifest at The Church of Jesus Christ of Latter-day Saints Missionary Training Centers. The fluency with which Latter-day Saints learn a foreign language can not be duplicated elsewhere in other programs and must be attributed to the Spirit. What happens at the Missionary Training Centers of the Church can be called miraculous.

Second, the gift of tongues can be manifest when persons are so endowed with the glory and power of God that they may speak the pure or Adamic language. Joseph Smith first heard the gift of tongues manifest this way when he met his successor Brigham Young in Kirtland in September of 1832. Joseph identified the language Brigham used on this occasion as "Adamic language." [45] The language of Adam and Eve has often been manifest in glossolalia in The Church of Jesus Christ of Latter-day Saints. In 1833, Joseph Smith made it clear that glossolalia was for both genders. While preaching to a small group in Ontario, Canada, he stopped and uttered, "If one of you will rise up and open your mouth it shall be filled and you shall speak in tongues. . . . Sister Lydia, rise up!" As she did "she was enveloped as with a flame, and her mouth was filled with the praises of God and his glory. The spirit of tongues was upon her." [46] Three years later, in 1836, as the Kirtland Temple was dedicated, the prayer contained a virtual plea for "the fulfillment of Joel's prophecy" and requested for the pronounced outpouring of the Spirit, "as upon those on the day of Pentecost." [47] During the dedication, there was a rich manifestation of the Spirit through spiritual gifts, including many who spoke in tongues. [48]

Third, when a person speaks under the influence of the Holy Ghost, they speak with the tongues of angels or they speak what God or his ministering servants would speak if they were present. This is also a manifestation of the gift of tongues.

Miracles &

The Beholding of Angels and Ministering Spirits

From the Book of Mormon, another pair of spiritual gifts are listed as "work[ing] mighty miracles" and "the beholding of angels and ministering spirits" (Moroni 10:12, 14). In the gospel of Jesus Christ, miracles are those occurrences wrought by the power of God which are beyond the ability and power of man to perform. Miracles appear as situations produced by supernatural power. Synonyms for the word miracle include marvels, wonders, and signs. [49] Most Latter-day Saints are aware of instances of miracles and the beholding of angels and ministering spirits taking place in the lives of members of The Church of Jesus Christ of Latter-day Saints. Such miracles are often too sacred to speak of in Sacrament meetings. Though not shared publicly, this does not mean miracles do not happen on a regular basis in the Lord's true Church. Elder Bruce R. McConkie explains, "If a man has power to part the veil and converse with angels and with the ministering spirits who dwell in the realms of light, surely this is a gift of the Spirit." [50] Elder Jeffrey R. Holland has identified the power to witness and perform miracles as the most dramatic of the spiritual gifts. [51]

By Identifying Less Conspicuous Gifts, We May Discover Our Own Gifts

Although Paul, Moroni, and Joseph Smith give us lists in the scriptures of spiritual gifts, these lists are not meant to be comprehensive or complete. There are many more spiritual gifts than those listed scripturally. Indeed, Apostle Bruce R. McConkie stated, "Spiritual gifts are endless in number and infinite in variety. Those listed in the revealed word are simply illustrations of the boundless outpouring of divine grace that a gracious God gives those who love and serve him." [52] Other gifts besides those found scripturally have been described by General Authorities. In October 1987, Elder Marvin J. Ashton, of the Quorum of the Twelve Apostles, listed gifts which he identified as less conspicuous. Elder Ashton said there are many gifts which are very real and most useful though they are "not always evident or noteworthy," but these gifts are extremely important in the lives of Latter-day Saints. Elder Ashton's list included:

Asking

Listening

Hearing and using a still small voice

Being able to weep

Avoiding contention

Being agreeable

Avoiding vain repetition

Seeking that which is righteous

Not passing judgment

Looking to God for guidance

Being a disciple

Caring for others

Being able to ponder

Offering prayer

Bearing a mighty testimony

Receiving the Holy Ghost

Elder Ashton gave some wonderful commentary explaining each of these "less-conspicuous gifts." Of those blessed with the gift of pondering he said, "We give the Spirit an opportunity to impress and direct. Pondering is a powerful link between heart and mind." Those who can ponder can read the scriptures and have their hearts and minds touched. Elder Ashton instructed, "If we use the gift to ponder we can take these eternal truths and realize how we can incorporate them into daily actions." Another gift he described was the "gift to hear and use the small voice. . . . Most often, hope, encouragement, and direction come from a soft, piercing voice. Small voices are heard only by those who are willing to listen. Soft and small voice communications with our associates make priceless friendships possible." Elder Ashton instructs, "I am appreciative of people who find no need to raise their voices as they try to impress or convince. It seems most people who argue and shout have ceased listening to what the small voice could powerfully contribute." Another unusual gift discussed by Elder Ashton is what he described as the "majestic gift to be able to calm others." As we have been told, "contention is a tool of the adversary." On the other hand, "Peace is a tool of the Savior," whereas, "contention stops progress. Argument and debate must be supplanted by calm discussion, study, listening and negotiation." The gospel of Jesus Christ "is one of harmony unity and agreement." Those with this spiritual gift conduct themselves with "calm assurance under all circumstances" and are not "manipulated or enraged by those who subtly foster contention over issues of the day." Another spiritual gift mentioned was the ability to care. Families, friends and organizations who care make life easier and more meaningful. Such gifts as listed above are not always thought of immediately as spiritual gifts but truly bless others lives and increase self-esteem. [53]

President Boyd K. Packer brought our attention to these less-known gifts:

> The gift of administration
>
> Seeing as seers see
>
> Revelation
>
> Discernment
>
> Visions
>
> Dreams
>
> Visitations
>
> Promptings
>
> Feelings
>
> Sensing whether a decision is right or wrong
>
> Gift of healing
>
> Warnings
>
> Raising the dead
>
> Gift of translation
>
> The gift to teach by the Spirit
>
> The Gift to be guided. [54]

President Packer described the gift of guidance as "when certain events happen (often small events in our lives) that could not possibly be coincidental, we get the impression that there is a Power and a Source that knew we would be there and what we would be about."[55]

Elder Robert C. Oaks suggests that we each have what he calls temporal gifts, that if uncovered and polished bring joy and satisfaction. Some of these temporal gifts he lists are an aptitude for music, for teaching, for learning, for athletics, or for administration and toleration for stress and capacity for work. Elder Oaks learned of some of his own temporal gifts while he was a college student. On one occasion, he shared:

> In high school I thought I was a pretty good athlete, and I wanted to play college ball. I went out for football . . . , promptly got cut. Then I went out for basketball, promptly got cut. I didn't bother with baseball and tennis, but I wasn't convinced of my limitations even though everyone else seemed to be fully aware of them.
>
> I went off to the Air Force academy. One of my driving factors was that I wanted another go at collegiate athletics. Now, with only 300 cadets on the campus at that time, odds were much better, so I played football, and basketball, and baseball my first year in Colorado. But my maturing interspection capacity, and knee surgery, made me realize that I was not quite mediocre on my better days. And based on that realization I made some adjustment to my life goals. And I have enjoyed a lifetime of participating in sports, but I was able to measure success and happiness in terms of participation rather than in terms of excellence in performance. . . . But through all this I did learn that I could work as hard as anyone. That was not a native skill. My dad taught me how to work. All of my life I've been able to keep up with the hardest workers. That became one of my most important lessons from my college life. Your successes highlight your gifts. Your disappointments highlight your limitations. And these are very important lessons that impact directly on who

you are in God's plan. These lessons play a major role
in helping you to determine your true identity. [56]

There are also those who possess social gifts that are sometimes less
conspicuous, such as cheerfulness, the ability to put people at ease,
and being able to counsel or lead. Many Latter-day Saints are gifted
and yet may not feel they are because their gifts are not identified in
the scriptures. Julie B. Beck, counselor in the general Young Women
presidency observed a uncommon gift of her mother as follows:

> When I was a little girl, I often experienced serious
> illness. My father was always willing and worthy to
> use the priesthood power he held to bless me. But I
> have also felt that my mother's special gifts contributed
> to my healing. She was truly gifted in her ability to
> minister to my needs and help me get well. Her great
> faith that the Lord would lead her to answers about
> medical treatment was a comfort to me. How blessed I
> was to have two parents who lovingly used their spiri-
> tual gifts. [57]

Such less conspicuous spiritual gifts as displayed by Sister Beck's
mother bless the lives of others just as much as those listed in the scriptures. Though they may not be mentioned in the standard works, such
gifts are of great importance to those who are recipients. Renowned
scholar Hugh Nibley, who blessed many lives, spoke of his less conspicuous gifts.

> I have always been furiously active in the church, but
> I have . . . never held any *office* or rank in anything; I
> have undertaken many assignments given me by the
> leaders, and much of the work has been anonymous;
> no rank, no recognition, no anything. While I have
> been commended for some things, they were never
> the things which I considered most important—that
> was entirely a little understanding between me and my
> Heavenly Father, which I have thoroughly enjoyed,
> though no one else knows anything about it. [58]

As Hugh Nibley described, the development of those private gifts
can lift our self-esteem, and studying both what has been said in the
scriptures and by our modern-day General Authorities will help us
identify our gifts.

Surrounding Ourselves with Refinement Cultivates Spiritual Gifts

Gifts of the Spirit are cultivated in the soil of refinement. In juxtaposition, when you and I associate with the base, crude, or brash we lose the ability to redevelop or display spiritual gifts. President Boyd K. Packer has declared that transgression, wickedness, apathy, indifference, and being caught up too much in the things of the world, "short circuit the possibility of receiving spiritual gifts."[59] The thirteenth article of faith describes the soil in which spiritual gifts grow:

> We believe in being honest, true, chaste, benevolent, virtuous, and in doing good to all men; indeed we may say that we follow the admonition of Paul—We believe in all things, we hope all things, and hope to be able to endure all things. If there is anything virtuous, lovely, or of good report or praiseworthy, we seek after these things.

When we focus our thoughts on uplifting things such as mentioned in this article of faith, we reap certain powers from the Holy Ghost. As the Lord has told Zion to arise and put on her beautiful garments, much of that adornment has to do with the spiritual gifts. "And awake, and arise from the dust, O Jerusalem; yea, and put on thy beautiful garments, O daughter of Zion; and strengthen thy stakes and enlarge thy borders forever, that thou mayest no more be confounded, that the covenants of the Eternal Father which he hath made unto thee, O house of Israel, may be fulfilled" (Moroni 10:31).

Early prophets of this dispensation envisioned Zion becoming refined as Latter-day Saints redevelop gifts and talents as never before. Joseph Young reported the Prophet Joseph Smith prophesying about musical gifts of Zion.

> The Saints [would] cultivate as high a state of perfection in their musical harmonies as the standard of the faith which he had brought was superior to sectarian religion. To obtain this, he gave them to understand that the refinement of singing would depend upon the attainment of the Holy Spirit.[60]

Brigham Young declared that "Every accomplishment, every polished grace, every useful attainment in mathematics, music, and in all sciences and art belong to the Saints."[61] Similarly, John Taylor envisioned that,

> [The Saints shall yet] rear splendid edifices, magnificent temples and beautiful cities that shall become the pride, praise and glory of the whole earth. We believe that this people will excel in literature, in science and the arts in manufactures. In fact, there will be a concentration of wisdom, not only of the combined wisdom of the world as it now exists, but men will be inspired in regard to all these matters in a manner and to an extent that they never have been before, and we shall have eventually, when the Lord's purposes are carried out, the most magnificent buildings, the most pleasant and beautiful gardens, the richest and most costly clothing, and be the most healthy and the most intellectual people that will reside upon the earth. This is part and parcel of our faith. . . . the people, from the President down, will all be under the guidance and direction of the Lord in all the pursuits of human life, until eventually they will be enabled to erect cities will be fit to be caught up—that when Zion descends from above, Zion will also ascend from beneath, and be prepared to associate with those from above. . . . This is the idea, in brief, that we have entertained in relation to many of these things.[62]

Understanding that what President John Taylor prophesied was possible, in 1977 modern prophet President Spencer W. Kimball gave a challenge he entitled "The Gospel Vision of the Arts." He pled with the Latter-day Saints to redevelop gifts to a degree which had never been experienced before. President Kimball mentioned some of the greatest musicians of all time such as Bach, Verdi, Caruso, Jenny Lind, Litz, Paginini, and Handel. He then stated that "deep in the throats of faithful Saints of today and tomorrow are superior qualities which, superbly trained, can equal or surpass these great known, musicians." He observed that there had not yet been composed or produced the greatest music, and he suggested that the greatest piece of music ever written would have the visit of Christ to the Americas as its subject.

President Kimball also mentioned George Bernard Shaw and the ability Latter-day Saints would have to write meaningful literature. He mentioned great statesman and begged the Saints "to know that art of statesmanship, to know people and conditions, to know situations and problems, . . . [to become] men who will be trained so thoroughly in the arts of their future work and in the basic honesties and integrities and spiritual concepts that there will be no compromise of principle." He also listed Da Vinci, Michelangelo, Goethe, and Rembrandt and said that for years, he had been waiting for someone to do justice in recording, in story, in painting, or in sculpture, the story of the Restoration. He talked to film makers and envisioned that they would "produce a master piece which would live forever." President Kimball ended this landmark address with the following:

> Take a Da Vinci or a Michelangelo or a Shakespeare and give him a total knowledge of the plan of salvation of God and personal revelation and cleanse him, and then take a look at the statues he will carve and the murals he will paint and the masterpieces he will produce. . . . In our world there have risen brilliant stars in drama, music literature, sculpture painting, science and all the graces. For long years I have had a vision of members of the Church greatly increasing their already strong positions of excellence till the eyes of all the world will be upon us.[63]

As the talents and gifts of Latter-day Saints are refined, the eyes of the world will be upon us and the Gospel will fill the whole earth. Moroni pleads with us, "deny not the gifts of God, for they are many; and they come from the same God" (Moroni 10:8). At the same time, Moroni promises us that "all these gifts . . . never will be done away, even as long as the world shall stand, only according to the unbelief of the children of men" (Moroni 10:19). Moroni ends his writings by warning, that those who do away with spiritual gifts will not be saved in the kingdom of God (Moroni 10:26).

If we redevelop and use our gifts as the Lord envisions we will be saved in the kingdom of God, and we will also become bearers of great self-esteem. As Elder Gene R. Cook has discovered,

> One of the great processes you go through in life is to discover yourself, to find those gifts and capacities

God has given you. He has given you great talents, the
smallest part of which you have just begun to utilize.
Trust the Lord to assist you in unlocking the door to
those gifts. Some of us have created imaginary limits
in our minds. There is literally a genius locked up
inside each of us. Don't ever let anyone convince you
otherwise. [64]

As we redevelop our spiritual gifts by studying our patriarchal
blessing, paying attention to compliments, accepting and fulfilling
callings, paying attention to promptings, studying gifts thereby recognizing our own as described in the scriptures, observing the less
conspicuous gifts, and surrounding ourselves with refinement, we will
unlock the genius in each of us.

1. Boyd K. Packer, *The Shield of Faith* (Salt Lake City: Bookcraft, 1998), 101–102.

2. Ibid., 106 and 99.

3. Hugh Nibley, *Approaching Zion*, volume 9 in the Collected Works of Hugh Nibley (Salt Lake City: Deseret
   Book, 1989), 89–90.

4. *Discourses of Brigham Young*, ed. John A. Widtsoe, (Salt
   Lake City: Bookcraft, 1998), 32.

5. George Q. Cannon, *The Latter-day Saints' Millennial Star*,
   Manchester, England: The Church of Jesus Christ of
   Latter-day Saints, 1840–1970, April 23, 1894, 56:260–
   261.

6. Bryant S. Hinckley, *Heber J. Grant: Highlights in the Life
   of a Great Leader* (Salt Lake City: Deseret Book, 1951),
   183–188.

7. *Teachings of Presidents of the Church: Heber J. Grant, 2: The
   Mission of the Prophet Joseph Smith, From the Life of Heber J.
   Grant*, 11. Taken from *Gospel Standards*, 368–70.

8. Joseph Smith, *History of The Church of Jesus Christ of Latter-
   day Saints*, ed. B.H. Roberts, 2nd ed. rev. (Salt Lake City:
   Deseret Book, 1978), 4:602, 604–605, and 607.

9. Bruce R. McConkie, *A New Witness for the Articles of Faith*, (Salt Lake City: Deseret Book, 1985), 369.

10. Harold B. Lee, *Stand Ye in Holy Places* (Salt Lake City: Deseret Book, 1975), 117.

11. Hartman and Connie Rector, *No More Strangers*, (Salt Lake City: Bookcraft, 1971), vol. 1, 33.

12. *Church News*, 12 October 1986, 2.

13. *Encyclopedia of Mormonism*, 4 vols. ed. Daniel H. Ludlow (New York: Macmillan, 1992), 1066.

14. *Teachings of Ezra Taft Benson*, 484–485, and "In His Steps," in 1979 Devotional Speeches of the Year (Provo: BYU, 1980), 64-65.

15. John A. Widtsoe, *Evidences and Reconciliations* (Salt Lake City: Bookcraft, 1960), 74–75.

16. Robert C. Oaks, "Understand Who You Are," Brigham Young University Devotional, 21 March 2006, 4.

17. James E. Faust, "Patriarchal Blessings," *New Era*, November 1982, 4 and 6.

18. *Encyclopedia of Mormonism*, 4 vols. ed. Daniel H. Ludlow (New York: Macmillan, 1992), 1354.

19. John Smith, Patriarchal Blessing to Joseph Fielding Smith, 19 January 1896; copy in LDS Church Historian's Library.

20. Patriarchal Blessing of Spencer W. Kimball, given by Patriarch Samuel Claridge when he was nine years of age, as quoted in Boyd K. Packer, "President Spencer W. Kimball: No Ordinary Man," *Ensign*, March 1974, 12.

21. Marion G. Romney, *BYU Speeches of the Year, 1963*, 3.

22. Carl W. Buehner, *BYU Speeches of the Year, 1960*, 4.

23. Bruce R. McConkie, *Doctrinal New Testament*, vol. 1 (Salt Lake City: Bookcraft, 1979), 689.

24. Neal A. Maxwell, "It's Service, Not Status, That Counts," *Ensign*, July 1975, 7.

25. Peter Marshall, *The Senate Prayers of Peter Marshall* (Sandwich, MA: Chapman Billies, Inc., 1996), 95.

26. Thomas S. Monson, "Choose You This Day," *Ensign*, November 2004, 67.

27. Joseph Smith, *Teachings of the Prophet Joseph Smith*, (Salt Lake City: Deseret Book, 1979), 51.

28. Ibid., 151.

29. Neal A. Maxwell, "Called to Serve," *Brigham Young University 1993-1994 Devotional and Fireside Speeches*, (Provo: Brigham Young University Press, 1994), 135 and 137.

30. Jeffrey Holland, *Christ and the New Covenant*, (Salt Lake City; Deseret Book, 1997), 324.

31. Brigham Young, *Journal of Discourses*, 26 vol. (London: Latter-day Saints Book Depot, 1854–86), 1:90.

32. Ibid., 9:141

33. Harold B. Lee, *The Teachings of Harold B. Lee*, ed. Clyde J. Williams (Salt Lake City: Bookcraft, 1996), 640.

34. Hyrum M. Smith and Janne M. Sjodahl, *Doctrine and Covenants Commentary*, (Salt Lake City: Deseret Book, 1978), 274.

35. J. Reuben Clark Jr., *Talk Tidbits*, comp. Albert L. Zobell Jr. (Salt Lake City: Bookcraft, 1972), 49–50.

36. B. H. Roberts, *History of the Church of Jesus Christ of Latter-day Saints*, (Salt Lake City: Deseret Book, 1978), 1:215–216.

37. Hyrum M. Smith and Janne M. Sjodahl, *Doctrine and Covenants Commentary* (Salt Lake City: Deseret Book, 1978), 275.

38. Orson F. Whitney, *The Life of Heber C. Kimball*, (Salt Lake City: Deseret Book, 2001), 389–391.

39. Joseph Fielding McConkie and Robert L. Millet, *Doctrinal Commentary on the Book of Mormon,* 4 vols. (Salt Lake City: Bookcraft, 1987–1992), 4:368.

40. Deseret News, July 30, 1862, 33 as quoted by Julie B. Beck, "An Outpouring of Blessings," *Conference Report*, April 2006.

41. Joseph Smith, "The Holy Ghost," *The Contributor* (May, 1882), 3:227.

42. Joseph Smith, *Teachings of the Prophet Joseph Smith*, comp. Joseph Fielding Smith (Salt Lake City: Deseret Book, 1938), 229.

43. John Taylor, *Journal of Discourses*, 26 vol. (London: Latter-day Saints Book Depot, 1854–86), 11:136.

44. Joseph Smith, *Teachings of the Prophet Joseph Smith*, comp. Joseph Fielding Smith (Salt Lake City: Deseret Book, 1938), 162.

45. *The Latter-day Saints' Millennial Star*, Manchester, England: The Church of Jesus Christ of Latter-day Saints, 1840–1970, vol. 25, 439.

46. *Journal History of the Church of Jesus Christ of Latter-day Saints, 1830–*, LDS Church Archives, Salt Lake City, 19 October 1833.

47. Alan K. Parish, "Your Daughters Shall Prophesy: A Latter-Day Prophecy of Joel, Peter, and Moroni Examined," *The Old Testament and the Latter-day Saints*, Sperry Symposium 1986 (Salt Lake City: Randall Book 1986), 283.

48. Ibid., 283, 286; D&C 109:35.

49. Bruce R. McConkie, *Mormon Doctrine*, 2nd ed. (Salt Lake City: Bookcraft, 1996), 506.

50. Bruce R. McConkie, *A New Witness for the Articles of Faith* (Salt Lake City: Deseret Book, 1985), 374.

51. Jeffrey R. Holland, *Christ and the New Covenant: The Messianic Message of the Book of Mormon* (Salt Lake City: Deseret Book, 1997), 333.

52. Bruce R. McConkie, *A New Witness for the Articles of Faith* (Salt Lake City: Deseret Book, 1985), 371.

53. Marvin J. Ashton, "There are Many Gifts," *Ensign*, November 1987, 20–23.

54. Boyd K. Packer, *The Shield of Faith* (Salt Lake City: Bookcraft, 1998), 96–97.

55. Ibid., 97.

56. Robert C. Oaks, "Understand Who You Are." Brigham Young University Devotional, 21 March 2006, 4–5.

57. Julie B. Beck, "An Outpouring of Blessings," *Conference Report*, April 2006.

58. Hugh Nibley, "The Best Possible Test," *Dialogue*, vol. 8 (1973): 75.

59. Boyd K. Packer, *The Shield of Faith* (Salt Lake City: Bookcraft, 1998), 107.

60. Joseph Young, "Vocal Music," in *History of the Organization of the Seventies*, (Salt Lake City: Deseret Stream Printing Establishment, 1878), 15.

61. Brigham Young, *Journal of Discourses*, 26 vol. (London: Latter-day Saints Book Depot, 1854–86), 10:224.

62. John Taylor, *Journal of Discourses*, 26 vol. (London: Latter-day Saints Book Depot, 1854–86), 10:147.

63. Spencer W. Kimball, "The Gospel Vision of the Arts," *Ensign*, July 1977, 3.

64. Gene R. Cook, *Hope* (Salt Lake City: Deseret Book, 1994), 90–91.

Chapter 10
Do It with
a Purpose

Life was difficult for Sally Bush Johnston. A widow with three children, she was getting old before her time. She suddenly saw a chance for an easier life when a suitor, whom she had known before she married and who now was a widower, came courting. Dressed in a fine suit and a new pair of boots, he spoke of prosperity, farming, servants and a way of life that seemed to be an improvement. Therefore, she married and went away with him.

> When she got [to his home], she found the "prosperous farm" to be a ramshackle, run-down farm. . . . The house was a floorless hut—a log cabin, in fact, without windows. The only evidence of servants was two small children, a boy and a girl.

> Her first thought was an obvious one: "I can't stay. . ." She knew she had been duped. But as she turned to leave, she looked at the children, especially the younger—a boy whose thin face and melancholy gaze made upon her soul an impression as deep as it was instantaneous. At that moment a great spirit subdued her disappointment. She slipped off her sweater and began to straighten and clean the house. In determined words that she felt deeply within her, she said quietly, "I'll stay for the sake of this boy."

> A neighbor was to write sometime later, "Oh Sally Bush, what a treasure trembled in the balance that

day." But Sally Bush could not have known that her stepson, this young boy whose melancholy eyes had penetrated her heart, was to become the President of the United States, states remaining "united" through a tragic civil war that would claim his life among the numbered dead. Sally Bush Lincoln, discouraged and tired and disappointed, looked into the eyes of a ten-year-old boy and said, "I'll stay for the sake of this boy." [1]

As Sally Lincoln blessed her stepson, she too was enlarged and will be remembered as Lincoln's "angel mother." At one point, Lincoln stated, "All that I am, or hope to be, I owe to my angel mother." [2] Likewise, as we help to develop and facilitate the gifts of others, we create opportunities, just as Sally Lincoln did for her young stepson. Consequently, our lives will also be blessed. As we willingly help others develop their gifts, there is a multiplying effect, and our own gifts come to the surface. Elder Robert C. Oaks promises that as we bless the lives of others through our gifts, in so doing we will bless our own lives. [3] For people who are willing to give of themselves that others may be blessed, there is great enlargement of spirit.

If we are to enlarge our own self-worth, our purpose in redeveloping our spiritual gifts must be rooted in blessing the lives of others. Seeking to gain spiritual gifts for any alternate reasons will not result in the growth of our own self-esteem. Rather, much will be lost in our own development. For example, striving for spiritual gifts cannot be motivated by fear of others. If we develop our talents to please and appease others, our subsequent sense of well-being will be limited. Nor can we try to increase spiritual gifts as a means to avoid legitimate responsibility elsewhere in our lives. For instance, a wife who over-commits to Relief Society duties at the expense of family obligations would no longer be serving the kingdom as much as she would be serving herself. We cannot strive to develop spiritual gifts at the expense of others, nor can we be motivated by the need for recognition and personal gain. "Service cannot be offered as a bid for receiving praise from others. Involvement in meetings through talks and prayers cannot be motivated out of a need to be recognized as someone knowledgeable or pious." [4] Such efforts would negate the development of self-esteem. As Elder Marlin K. Jensen of the First Quorum of the Seventy divulged,

"Those who seek honor and gain for themselves in doing the Lord's work are guilty of what the scriptures call priestcrafts."[5] Our outward spiritual activity should not accompany an inward spiritual emptiness. Our spirits will acknowledge this as incongruity and deception. If our behavior is incongruent with our desires, increased activity (such as more meeting attendance, more scripture study, or more service) will not create more self-acceptance. While such activity is worthwhile, it cannot replace a desire to bless others.[6] The purpose of spiritual gifts is not to create self-esteem but rather to bless others. Self-esteem simply comes as a by-product of that service.

One of the most endearing songs of the nineteenth century came as a husband sought to bless his wife's life. In turn, his talents were developed, and his name became known for generations as a renowned poet.

> Thomas Moore, a famous nineteenth century Irish poet, . . . [once] returned from a business trip [and] found his wife had locked herself in her upstairs bedroom and had asked to see no one. Moore learned the terrible truth that his beautiful wife had contracted smallpox and her milky complexion was now pocked and scarred. She had looked at herself in the mirror and demanded that the shutters be drawn, and that she never see her husband again. Thomas Moore did not listen. He went upstairs to the darkened room and started to light the lamp. His wife pleaded with him to let her remain in darkness alone. She felt it best not to subject her husband to seeing his loved one with her beauty marred. She asked him to go.

> Moore did not go. He went downstairs and spent the rest of the night in prayerful writing. He had never written a song before, but that night he wrote not only words, but also composed music. As daylight broke, Moore returned to his wife's darkened room. "Are you awake?" he asked.

> "Yes," she said, "but you must not see me. Please don't press me, Thomas."

"I'll sing to you then," he said. Thomas More sang to his wife the song that still lives today.

> *Believe me, if all those endearing young charms*
> *Which I gaze on so fondly today,*
> *Were to change by tomorrow and fleet in my arms,*
> *Like fairy gifts fading away,*
> *Thou wouldst still be adored as this moment thou art*

Moore heard a movement in the corner of the darkened room where his wife lay in loneliness. He continued:

> *Let thy loveliness fade as it will,*
> *And around the dear ruin each wish of my heart*
> *Would entwine itself verdantly still.*

The song ended. As his voice faded, Moore heard his bride arise. She crossed the room to the window, reached up and slowly withdrew the shutters, opened the curtain, and let in the morning light.[7]

Most of us will rediscover the gifts we brought with to this life, but unfortunately, many of us will not use them, as Sir Thomas Moore did, to bless those around us.

How different from the lens of history is our view of Thomas Moore than the view of one seventy-year old man who, looking back on his life, described his "whole life [as] a succession of disappointments." At one point he divulged, "I can scarcely recollect a single instance of success in anything that I ever undertook."[8] These words were spoken by a person whose life would not historically be thought of as a disappointment. Ironically, the man who spoke these words served as member of the United States Congress, as a Foreign Ambassador, and as the sixth president of the United States. With such accomplishments, one might wonder why John Quincy Adams would characterize his life so harshly. Though I can only speculate, I wonder if John Quincy Adams accomplished these feats without the intent of blessing other's lives. Perhaps his accomplishments were devoid of the true purpose of sharing talents. If, in the beginning and middle, we selfishly hoard our talents for our own personal self-aggrandizement, developing spiritual gifts will leave us devoid of self-esteem in the end. Sometimes there are even people who use their talents and capacities to put down others. Christ, who possesses every spiritual gift, always uses His gifts to lift others. His great example teaches us about the purpose of spiritual gifts and instructs us how to render them useful.

Camilla Eyring Kimball instructs how to correctly use our talents as follows:

> To be rich is good, if you can be humble. To be learned is good if you can be wise. To be healthy is good if you can be useful. To be beautiful is good if you can be gracious.
>
> There is, however, nothing inherently bad in being poor, unlettered, sickly, or plain.
>
> To be poor is good, if you can still be generous of spirit. To be unschooled is good, if it motivates you to be curious. To be sickly is good, if it helps you to have compassion. To be plain is good, if it saves you from vanity. [9]

As Camilla Kimball so beautifully outlined, much can be good if our attitudes and motives have others in mind. Likewise, exercising spiritual gifts can bring about much good if it is to lift others. The Lord instructed: "And again, verily I say unto you, I would that ye should always remember, and always retain in your minds what those gifts are, that are given unto the church. For all have not every gift given unto them; for there are many gifts, and to every man is given a gift by the Spirit of God. To some is given one, and to some is given another, that all may be profited thereby" (D&C 46:11–12).

When we truly love God, the cruel constrains of ego release us, and those around us profit from associating with us. Following our Heavenly Father's example, our real selves will seek opportunities to influence others for good with our spiritual gifts rather than force others to change. [10] If we develop and use our gifts as the Lord envisioned, we will become bearers of great self-acceptance. When the spiritual gifts are developed with the purpose of helping others, we will become what Parley P. Pratt describes as follows:

> An intelligent being, in the image of God, [who] possesses every organ, attribute, sense, sympathy, affection that is possessed by God himself. . . . The gift of the

Holy Ghost adapts itself to all these organs or attributes. It quickens all the intellectual faculties, increases,
enlarges, expands and purifies all the natural passions
and affections, and adapts them, by the gift of wisdom,
to their lawful use. It inspires, develops, cultivates and
matures all the fine toned sympathies, joys, kindness,
goodness, tenderness, gentleness and charity. It develops beauty of person, form and features. It tends to
health, vigor, animations, and social feelings. It invigorates all the faculties of the physical and intellectual
man. It strengthens, invigorates and gives tone to the
nerves. In short, it is, as it were, marrow to the bone,
joy to the heart, light to the eyes, music to the ears,
and life to the whole being. [11]

Such individuals bless others simply by being in their presence. These
intelligent beings made in the image of God are filled with spiritual
gifts and, as a result are also filled with self-approval.

That self-approval depends in part on our ability to act in congru-
ence with our "internal/external identity, that part of us that lived
with God and learned the difference between right and wrong." [12]
Our eternal identities resonate all that is good about us, including our
spiritual gifts. Our spirits chose the Savior's plan in the premortal existence, and they can direct our choices now and help us bless lives with
our talents. In this way, self-approval results from heeding to our spirits
that receive truth directly from an eternal source. "There is no greater
self-approval than the self-approval that comes from doing what we
know is pleasing to the Lord," and remembering and redeveloping our
spiritual gifts to bless others will please Him. [13]

As we redevelop faith, hope, charity, and myriad other unique
and individual spiritual gifts, our self-esteem will be enhanced. Self-
esteem will manifest itself in our capacity to love ourselves and love
others more fully. As Bednar and Peterson explain, "Self-esteem is
a barometer that tells us, as well as anybody else who cares to look,
whether we have a truly durable, internal sense of personal well-being,
a well-being that leads to a quiet confidence and self-assuredness. Even
though self-esteem is a temporal, psychological concept, it is far from
a trivial spiritual matter, given that the second great commandment
instructs us to love our neighbors as we love ourselves." [14] Rather than

simply adding the acquisition of spiritual gifts to a long list of things to do, spiritual gifts can become the template that guides the doing. "Personal accomplishments are much less important than personal integrity, which itself guides achievement. The character we display and the Christ-like qualities we exemplify, become embedded in the choices we make, the relationships we cultivate, and the many small behaviors that make up our larger lives."[15]

Our possession of spiritual gifts will largely determine our degree of happiness in this life. If we possess faith, hope, and charity, we will have an internal well-being and self-appreciation that will last eternally. We will function here and in the hereafter fully, freely, and effectively in every facet of our lives. Mortality will be filled with high expectations for success and emotional security. If we rediscover our spiritual gifts, we will experience more happiness, more success, and more confidence and will bless those around us to experience the same. Our self-confidence will be more than a thought or belief. It will be a feeling that is constant in our day-to-day lives. In short, the possession of spiritual gifts will be joyous and life giving to us as we anticipate godhood. With the spiritual gifts as part of our eternal identities, we will leave mortality with a celestial self-esteem imbedded; and, when we meet our Savior, we will recognize Him, for we will appear as He, who is the giver of all spiritual gifts.

1. J. Richard Clarke, "The Royal Road to Happiness," *Hope* (Salt Lake City: Deseret Book, 1988), 137–138.

2. Josiah Gilbert Holland, *Life of Abraham Lincoln* (Springfield: Guerdon Bill, 1866), 23.

3. Robert C. Oaks, "Understand Who You Are." Brigham Young University Devotional, 21 March 2006, 4.

4. Richard L. Bednar and Scott R. Peterson, *Spirituality and Self-Esteem: Developing the Inner Self* (Salt Lake City: Deseret Book, 1990), 128.

5. Marlin K. Jensen, "An Eye Single to the Glory of God," *Ensign*, November 1989, 27.

6. Richard L. Bednar and Scott R. Peterson, *Spirituality and Self-Esteem: Developing the Inner Self* (Salt Lake City: Deseret Book, 1990), 129.

7. Robert D. Hales, "We Can't Do It Alone," *Ensign*, November 1975, 92.

8. As quoted in John F. Kennedy, *Profiles in Courage*, (New York: Harper, 1956), 35.

9. Camilla E. Kimball, "The Rewards of Correct Choices," *Ye Are Free to Choose: Agency and the Latter-day Saint Woman*, ed. Maren M. Mouritsen (Provo: Brigham Young University Publications, 1981), 18.

10. Garth L. Allred, *Unlocking the Powers of Faith* (American Fork: Covenant Communications, 1993), 91.

11. *Key to the Science of Theology* 5th ed. (Salt Lake City: George Q. Cannon & Sons, 1891), 101–102.

12. Richard L. Bednar and Scott R. Peterson, *Spirituality and Self-Esteem: Developing the Inner Self* (Salt Lake City: Deseret Book, 1990), 51.

13. Ibid., 51.

14. Ibid., 66.

15. Ibid., 131.

About the Author

Dr. Mary Jane Woodger is an associate professor of Church history and doctrine at Brigham Young University. Born and raised in American Fork and Salt Lake City, Utah, Dr. Woodger has always had a great love for teaching. After obtaining a B.S. in home economics education, Dr. Woodger taught home economics and American history in Salt Lake City, where she received the Vocational Teacher of the Year Award from Jordan School District. In 1992, she completed her M.Ed. at Utah State University. In 1997, she received from Brigham Young University an Ed.D. in Educational Leadership, with a minor in Church history and doctrine.

Kappa Omicron Nu honored Dr. Woodger in 1998 with an award of excellence for her dissertation research entitled, "The Educational Ideals of David O. McKay." Dr. Woodger has authored and co-authored numerous articles on doctrinal, historical, and educational subjects. These articles have appeared in various academic journals, as well as venues for the LDS audience including the *Journal of Book of Mormon Studies*, *Church News*, *Ensign*, and *The Religious Educator*. Her current research interests include twentieth century Church history, Latter-day Saint women's history, and Church education.